The Courtesan Killing That Divided 19th-Century New York

PUBLISHED BY: Ricky Indrawan

Dedication Page

For the women whose beauty became both their power and their peril.

For those who were touched not with tenderness, but with entitlement.
For the girls who reinvented themselves in a world that never forgave reinvention.

For the daughters who left small towns behind, only to find their names whispered behind closed doors.

To Helen Jewett—not a scandal, not a cautionary tale, but a young woman who once loved, dreamed, and dared to live on her own terms.

And to every reader who turns these pages not for thrill, but for reckoning—for truth buried beneath shame, for voices buried beneath reputation.

May we read not to consume her story, but to understand it. May we remember her not as a tragedy, but as a human being who deserved to grow old.

—Ricky Indrawan

Acknowledgements

This book began with the smoke rising from a locked room on Thomas Street. But it became much more than a story of violence—it became a story about the women history tried to erase, and the systems that chose to protect power over truth.

To my family—thank you for enduring the long nights of research and silence, for reminding me to rest even as I followed Helen's shadow across broadsheets and courtroom records. Your love made this possible.

To my research collaborators and editorial team—your relentless attention to detail, historical nuance, and narrative rhythm gave this book its spine. You helped me carry Helen with dignity and precision. You asked the hard questions so the reader wouldn't have to carry doubt alone.

To the archivists and librarians at the New York Public Library, the New-York Historical Society, and Chronicling America—you are the unseen heroes of every truth-teller. Your commitment to preservation made this resurrection of voice and memory possible.

To Patricia Cline Cohen, whose scholarship illuminated Helen's world with respect and rigor—thank you for proving that history and empathy can coexist.

To the readers—thank you for refusing to look away, for resisting easy answers, and for recognizing that even in the oldest unsolved cases, justice still matters. Your questions keep stories like Helen's alive.

And to Helen Jewett—this is for you. Not for who the newspapers said you were, or who the courtroom allowed you to be, but for the woman you were becoming. You were more than a body in a bed. You were a life interrupted. And you are not forgotten.

Caution!

Due to the graphic nature of this murder case, reader discretion is advised. This book includes dramatizations and discussions of sensitive topics such as gore, sex work, murder, and assault.

The content may be disturbing to some readers, as it delves into the darker aspects of human behaviour and societal issues that are often uncomfortable to confront.

We advise extreme caution for children under 13, as the themes explored in this narrative may not be suitable for younger audiences.

The narrative presented is not merely a recounting of events; it serves as a reflection on the human experience and the struggles faced by individuals in difficult circumstances.

As you engage with this material, please be aware of your own emotional responses and the potential impact of the subject matter.

If you find the content overwhelming or distressing, we encourage you to take breaks and prioritize your well-being. It is important to approach these discussions with care and understanding, recognizing the complexities of the issues involved.

Table of Contents

Helen Jewett

Case File

The Murder of Helen Jewett

1. Victim Profile

- **Name**: Helen Jewett (birth name: Dorcas Doyen)

- **Age at Death**: 23

- **Aliases Used**: Helen Jewett, Maria Stanley

- **Place of Birth**: Temple, Maine

- **Family**: Estranged from parents; orphaned young

- **Occupation**: Courtesan working under madam Rosina Townsend

- **Physical Description**: Tall, elegant, with auburn hair and pale skin; known for literary flair in her writing and emotional intensity in her relationships

- **Known Personality Traits**:

  - Intelligent and self-taught

- Maintained correspondence with multiple clients
- Alternated between romantic hopefulness and financial desperation

---

2. Identification and Recognition

- **Identified by**:
  - Rosina Townsend (madam of the brothel and employer)
  - Personal letters found in her trunk
  - Items of clothing, including nightdress and bonnet

- **Public Recognition**:
  - Widely known in New York's vice circuits under the name Helen Jewett
  - Frequently mentioned in anonymous gossip columns prior to her death

---

3. Discovery of the Crime

- **Date Discovered**: April 10, 1836

- **Time of Discovery**: Approximately 3:00 AM

- **Location**: Room No. 3, 41 Thomas Street, Manhattan (a known brothel)

- **Discovered by**:
  - Rosina Townsend, who noticed smoke under Helen's door
  - She unlocked the door and found Helen's body burning on the bed

- **Scene Details**:
  - Helen's body was partially burned, mostly around her head and chest
  - She had sustained a fatal head injury, believed to be from a hatchet
  - The bedsheets were blood-soaked and scorched

13

- A bloody hatchet was later found under the bed

---

4. Physical and Forensic Evidence

- **Blunt Force Injury:**

  - A large wound to the left temple, likely inflicted by a sharp hatchet

  - The blow was forceful enough to render her unconscious or kill her instantly

- **Post-Mortem Fire:**

  - Fire was set near the head and upper chest

  - Nightdress and linens were charred

  - Believed to be an attempt to destroy evidence

- **Recovered Objects:**

  - A bloodied hatchet

  - A black cloak later identified as belonging to the suspect

- Multiple handwritten letters and personal effects found in a locked trunk

- **Room Condition**:

  - Door was locked from the **inside**

  - No clear signs of forced entry

  - No scream was reported by other residents, possibly due to timing or shock

---

5. Prime Suspect

- **Name**: Richard P. Robinson

- **Alias Used**: Frank Rivers

- **Age**: 19

- **Occupation**: Clerk in a prestigious Wall Street law firm

- **Known Relationship to Victim**:

  - Repeated client of Helen Jewett

  - Maintained correspondence; several of his letters found among her belongings

- **Evidence Linking Him to the Crime**:
    - Booked the room under a false name
    - A black cloak traced to his person was found bloodied near the scene
    - Witness accounts suggested he was seen entering the premises
    - He provided a questionable alibi via his roommate, James Tew

---

6. Key Individuals

1. **Rosina Townsend** – Brothel madam and first witness to the crime scene

2. **James Tew** – Robinson's roommate, gave conflicting statements during investigation

3. **Ogden Hoffman** – Defense attorney for Robinson, known for attacking Helen's reputation

4. **James Gordon Bennett** – Editor of *The New York Herald*, played a central role in media coverage

16

5. **George Marston ("Bill Easy")** – Another client of Helen, possible rival of Robinson

6. **James R. Whiting** – Prosecutor, struggled to push a case against a socially protected defendant

7. **Police and Watchmen** – Initial law enforcement response, lacked forensic protocols of later eras

---

7. Timeline of Key Events

1. **April 9, 1836 (Evening)** – Helen receives her final client; believed to be Robinson under the alias "Frank Rivers"

2. **April 10, 1836 (Early Morning)** – Body discovered by Rosina Townsend

3. **April 11–12, 1836** – Robinson questioned and cloak discovered; initial inquest begins

4. **April 25, 1836** – Formal charges brought against Richard Robinson

5. **June 2–5, 1836** – Criminal trial held in New York City courtroom

6. **June 5, 1836** – Jury deliberates for 15 minutes; Robinson is acquitted

7. **Post-trial (1836–1837)** – Robinson flees public life; Helen's reputation publicly dismantled

8. **Later 1830s** – Public interest fades; no additional suspects pursued

---

8. Core Investigative Questions

- How did the killer exit a room locked from the inside?

- Was the fire set to obscure identity or destroy evidence?

- Did Richard Robinson receive special protection because of his class?

- Why did the jury dismiss strong circumstantial evidence and witness statements?

- Were there others involved in the killing—or in its cover-up?

- Why were Helen's moral choices more scrutinized than the accused's actions?

---

9. Legal Outcome

- **Charge**: First-degree murder (Richard P. Robinson)

- **Trial Dates**: June 2–5, 1836

- **Trial Result**: **Acquitted** after 15-minute jury deliberation

- **Post-Verdict Consequences**:

  o Robinson relocated and rebranded himself in the South

  o No further legal action taken against other suspects or witnesses

  o Helen Jewett was publicly vilified in post-trial media

---

10. Archival Sources and Documentation

- *The New York Herald*, April–June 1836 (editorials by James Gordon Bennett)

  https://chroniclingamerica.loc.gov/

- Patricia Cline Cohen, *The Murder of Helen Jewett*, Harvard University Press

  https://www.hup.harvard.edu/books/9780679740 759

- Court records (partial), New York State Archives

- New York Historical Society: Special Collections (letters and trial press clippings)

- JSTOR: "Helen Jewett and the American Tabloid Birth"

11. Summary

Despite public outrage and extensive press coverage, the murder of Helen Jewett was never officially solved. The court's focus on Helen's morality, rather than forensic and testimonial evidence, exemplified the era's gender and class prejudice. Her story was consumed by readers, debated by journalists, and buried beneath sensationalism. Today, her case endures not just as an unsolved crime—but as a reflection of how easily justice falters when respect is reserved for the privileged, not the slain.

Documented Chronology

Compiled from contemporary press articles, surviving court records, police documents, and postwar historical analysis

---

Early Life and Reinvention

- **October 18, 1813** – Dorcas Doyen is born in Temple, Maine, to working-class parents.

- **1820s** – As a child, Dorcas shows signs of intellectual ability and precociousness. She is orphaned young and taken in by a local judge, where she receives an informal education.

- **Late 1820s–early 1830s** – She leaves home and adopts the name "Helen Jewett" as she moves through various northeastern cities, including Portland and Boston, eventually settling in New York City.

- **1834–1836** – Helen gains notoriety in New York's sex work circles. She becomes known for her elegance, writing talent, and selective client list.

Lead-Up to the Murder

- **Early 1836** – Helen develops a close but volatile relationship with Richard P. Robinson, a teenage law clerk who frequents brothels under the alias "Frank Rivers."

- **March–April 1836** – Tensions rise between Helen and Robinson. Letters suggest jealousy, possible threats, and emotional turmoil.

- **April 5–9, 1836** – Helen reportedly expresses unease to Rosina Townsend and others, fearing one of her clients may be dangerous.

The Night of the Murder

- **April 9, 1836 (late evening)** – A man identified by Rosina Townsend as Richard Robinson visits 41 Thomas Street and requests to see Helen.

- **April 10, 1836 (approximately 3:00 a.m.)** – Smoke is seen coming from under Helen's locked door. Rosina Townsend and another girl force entry and find Helen's body burning on the bed, her head gashed.

- **3:30–4:00 a.m.** – A watchman is summoned. Initial accounts are chaotic. A bloody hatchet is discovered near the scene.

- **Morning of April 10, 1836** – Richard Robinson is arrested based on circumstantial evidence and witness testimony.

Investigation and Legal Proceedings

- **April 11–20, 1836** – Police collect statements. Robinson's cloak is found with bloodstains. Letters between Helen and Robinson are uncovered.

- **April 25, 1836** – Robinson is formally charged with the murder of Helen Jewett.

- **May 1836** – Public fascination escalates. *The New York Herald* begins publishing lurid and sympathetic coverage of Robinson.

- **June 2–5, 1836** – Robinson's trial takes place. Rosina Townsend testifies to seeing him enter the house that night. Defense attorney Ogden Hoffman attacks Helen's morality.

- **June 5, 1836** – After just 15 minutes of deliberation, the jury acquits Robinson. He leaves the courtroom a free man.

Immediate Aftermath

- **June–July 1836** – Outrage erupts in New York. Letters to editors and public commentary criticize the verdict. Townsend is publicly ridiculed.

- **Late 1836** – Robinson leaves New York and begins a new life in the South under his birth name.

- **1837–1839** – The case fades from national headlines. Helen's name is increasingly used as a symbol of moral decay rather than injustice.

Lingering Doubts and Historical Debate

- **1840s–1850s** – Periodicals occasionally revisit the case, but often frame it as a morality tale rather than a miscarriage of justice.

- **1880s–1900s** – The case is re-examined in retrospectives on sensational trials and the rise of tabloid journalism.

- **1998** – Historian Patricia Cline Cohen publishes *The Murder of Helen Jewett*, offering a scholarly reconsideration of the case and its gendered biases.

- **2000s–2020s** – Helen's story is cited in feminist studies, media ethics coursework, and true crime histories as a foundational case of reputation-driven justice failure.

Legacy

- **Today** – The murder of Helen Jewett remains one of the most infamous unsolved cases in early American criminal history. It is remembered not only for its brutality but for how it revealed the deep entanglement of gender, class, media, and power in shaping narratives of guilt and innocence.

Prologue

New York City – April 10, 1836

The night was warm for April. Fog rolled down the alleys of lower Manhattan like a curtain from an unseen stage, curling around gas lamps and dissolving into the shadows between buildings. On Thomas Street, the brick façade of Number 41 stood quiet—just another brothel nestled discreetly among the print shops, boardinghouses, and taverns of the city's Third Ward.

Inside, the house had already begun to drift into sleep. The girls had seen their final callers. Boots were off. Candles were guttering low. In the back parlor, Rosina Townsend, the house's madam, stirred from a light doze in her chair. Something had pulled her from sleep—a scent. Something acrid and wrong.

Smoke.

She sat upright, her pulse suddenly hammering. The scent was faint, but unmistakable. Burning fabric. She crossed the hallway barefoot, her nightdress whispering against the floorboards. The smoke was coming from Helen's room. Room No. 3.

She tapped on the door. No answer. Then she tried the knob.

Locked.

"Helen?" she called, her voice louder now. "Hclen, open this door!"

Still nothing. She shouted for help. Another girl came running. Together, they forced the door open—slamming into it until the wood cracked and splintered, until the lock gave way.

The room inside was filled with smoke. A candle had fallen. The bed was smoldering. And on it, barely visible through the haze, lay the twisted figure of a woman—her head bloodied, her nightgown scorched, her legs drawn up in a fetal curl.

Rosina screamed. She reached for a shawl and began batting at the flames, but it was too late. The fire had done its damage.

The body was Helen Jewett.

The city awoke the next morning to a sensation. *A Murder in a House of Ill Repute!* cried the *New York Sun*. *Brutal Courtesan Slaying Stuns the Third Ward*, declared the *Evening Post*.

Within hours, the crowds had gathered outside 41 Thomas Street—men in top hats and boys hawking penny papers, girls whispering behind gloved hands. By nightfall, Helen Jewett had gone from a quiet beauty in a brothel to the most talked-about woman in New York.

She would also become one of its most mythologized victims.

Helen Jewett, born Dorcas Doyen in a small town in Maine, had remade herself in the image of a romantic heroine.

With auburn hair, a sharp wit, and a taste for literature, she moved through parlors and bedrooms like a woman made of secrets. Men paid for her company, but she gave away nothing. Not truly.

By 1836, she had already lived many lives. Orphan. Servant. Courtesan. She was both admired and despised—by the men who desired her and the society that condemned her.

Now, she was dead. Murdered in the early hours of a Sunday morning, her skull split by a hatchet, her bed set ablaze. The fire hadn't destroyed the evidence—it had preserved it. The blood soaked into the mattress. The wound to her head. The door locked from the inside.

And a name whispered in horror by those who knew her: **Richard Robinson**.

A boy of just nineteen. A law clerk from a respected firm. Clean-cut, educated, well-connected. He'd courted Helen under the alias "Frank Rivers." His letters to her had been passionate, veiled, and full of possessive undertones.

He would soon become the only suspect. And by the end of that summer, he would also walk free.

Helen's murder marked more than the end of a life. It marked the beginning of something darker—an era in which class, gender, and the hunger for scandal would warp the pursuit of justice.

As the editor James Gordon Bennett wrote in his first detailed account of the case:

"Her death is not simply a tragedy—it is a mirror, held up to the city's face, showing us what we pretend not to see."
— *The New York Herald*, April 1836

The mirror was cracked. And the reflection was not flattering.

In the weeks to come, Helen would be dissected in print—her reputation slashed as cruelly as her body had been. Reporters would focus on her profession. Lawyers would argue her virtue. The courtroom would become a stage where one woman's murder was less important than her past.

And her killer—whoever he was—would vanish into history.

Not because he was never named.

But because Helen Jewett was never seen as worth the justice she deserved.

PART I -

A Room in Flames

Theme: Discovery of the murder, shock of the moment, the fragility of life under firelight

The story begins in silence—but not the kind that brings peace. It is the hush before horror, the breath held in the moment before the world changes. In the early hours of April 10, 1836, in a small, second-story room of a brothel on Thomas Street in Manhattan's Third Ward, that silence shattered. Smoke curled under a locked bedroom door. A scream tore through the walls. And when the door was broken open, the flames revealed not just a burning bed— but a body.

This was not the kind of crime the city could ignore. Helen Jewett was no common figure. Her life—shrouded in elegance, secrecy, and contradiction—demanded attention even in death. Beautiful, literate, and unrepentant in her profession, she occupied a space the city could not name:

not merely a prostitute, but a courtesan who moved among lawyers, clerks, and merchants as both lover and listener. She had risen far from her obscure beginnings in Maine and reinvented herself in New York's shadows, where money and morality walked hand in hand down unmarked streets.

In Part I, we follow the immediate aftermath of the murder through a cinematic lens—moment by moment, footstep by footstep—as the small house on Thomas Street descends into chaos. From the creaking floorboards to the flickering candlelight, from Rosina Townsend's trembling hands as she opens the scorched door to the stillness of Helen's broken body, the reader is brought directly into the moment. Not as a voyeur. But as a witness. Because to understand Helen's death, we must first confront the scene exactly as it was found.

The forensic evidence—or lack of it—tells its own story. There were no security patrols, no formal detectives in 1836 New York. The crime scene was compromised almost immediately. Yet even in that early morning fog of panic and disbelief, certain details stood out. The room was locked from the inside. Blood pooled beneath the bed and stained the mattress in thick, arterial bursts. A bloody hatchet was found at the scene. Helen's head bore three wounds—deliberate, clean, and terrifying in their finality.

As dawn broke and word spread, the city's attention turned swiftly to the house. Reporters arrived before the coroner. Neighbors gathered in clusters along the curb, whispering theories before the investigation had even begun. In their midst stood Rosina Townsend, the madam of the house—a woman caught between silence and survival. Her reputation, her livelihood, even her freedom were now at risk. And still she spoke. She named the man who had come to see Helen that night. A young law clerk named Richard Robinson.

The chapters in Part I do more than narrate events—they reconstruct a fragile world on the brink of collapse. The brothel itself becomes a character: 41 Thomas Street, a narrow house with a parlor lined in velvet, bedrooms furnished in mahogany and floral wallpaper, a back stairway often used for discretion. This was a place that thrived not in shame, but in secrecy. A place where women like Helen were both safe and never truly protected.

Helen's room was always immaculately arranged—her books neatly stacked, her ink bottle capped, her perfume faint but distinct. After her death, those same objects were cataloged not as traces of a life, but as potential evidence. A nightgown, half-burned. A diary, its pages filled with fine script and coded names. A comb with a strand of auburn hair still caught in its teeth. In retelling these details, we return agency to the victim. We allow her room to breathe before it becomes a courtroom exhibit.

This section also introduces the first contradictions. Witness accounts diverge. Some say Helen was expecting a visitor. Others claim she was fearful, anxious. One girl swore she heard arguing. Another heard nothing at all. The house may have kept its secrets—but the city would not. And the question that echoed louder than all others was simple: how had a man entered a locked room, committed a murder, and vanished into the fog?

Part I does not answer this question. Instead, it teaches the reader how to ask it. Through layered detail and sensory precision, the reader learns what investigators saw—and what they missed. We examine the position of Helen's body. The location of the murder weapon. The trail of ash and embers that led nowhere. We enter the limitations of 1836 policing, where gut instinct and public opinion often outweighed science. Where justice was not blind—it was selective.

Throughout this section, the writing walks the fine line between beauty and brutality. The language evokes not just what was done to Helen, but what her death revealed about the world around her. The fragility of a woman's life when her worth was defined by men. The way fire can both destroy evidence and illuminate truths. The price of living outside society's boundaries, and the even higher cost of dying there.

In the end, this part is not about Helen's death—it's about its discovery. The literal and metaphorical opening of a door. The rush of smoke and panic that follows. The city's reaction, the press's appetite, and the beginning of a national fascination with crime that would shape journalism—and public justice—for centuries to come.

"A Room in Flames" is where everything begins. With a locked door, a rising column of smoke, and a woman whose name history tried to reduce to scandal. Here, we restore her to the center. We let the scene speak. And we prepare the reader to walk through that smoke not just as a reader—but as an investigator.

Chapter 1:

Fire in the Dark

The stillness of Thomas Street was the kind only found in that thin stretch of night where Saturday ends and Sunday hasn't quite begun. It was April 10, 1836. New York's markets had closed, carriages had vanished, and the clamor of merchants and newsboys had given way to a hush broken only by the occasional rattle of wheels or the shuffle of a nightwatchman's step. Somewhere in the Third Ward, a dog barked once and fell silent. Just beyond the streetlamps' reach, smoke began to curl from behind a shuttered second-story window.

Inside number 41, a narrow brothel kept under the careful watch of Rosina Townsend, the air was thick with still-burning candles and stale perfume. The girls were asleep or pretending to be—doors shut, curtains drawn, earnings hidden in the hems of dresses. Then came the sound. A thud. The breaking of glass. A strange silence. And then— the unmistakable scent of fire.

It was a chambermaid who noticed it first. She crept into the hallway, trailing her nightdress, and screamed. Within moments, Rosina Townsend stood at the door to Helen Jewett's room, her heart slamming in her chest. The handle was warm. She called Helen's name once. No reply. She knocked again, harder, her knuckles reddening.

Still nothing.

She turned to another girl—a younger one—and shouted for help. Within moments, a handful of the women had gathered with blankets and pails, trying the door. It was locked. Smoke rolled beneath the threshold now, black and heavy. They hesitated. Then, together, they forced it open.

What they found would linger in their minds for the rest of their lives.

The room was dense with smoke, its wallpaper curling at the edges from the heat. The fire had not yet engulfed the space but had turned one corner of the bed into char. A figure lay atop it, face-down, unmoving. Her nightgown was scorched, and her hair, once the color of polished copper, was now a tangled, smoldering mess.

41

Rosina stepped back. She knew that body. The curve of the spine, the pale arm dangling from the edge of the bed—it was Helen. She was dead.

They smothered the flames with quilts and pulled back the sheets. The horror deepened. Her skull had been cleaved. Three neat gashes split the back of her head, blood now blackened by smoke. Her feet were bare. One leg dangled off the side. The air stank of burnt flesh and lamp oil.

"Get the watch," Rosina said hoarsely. "Now."

Within the hour, the police were on the scene. Watchmen from the neighborhood had gathered in confusion. The brothel, long ignored or tolerated, was now swarming with boots and questions. Rosina pointed to the blood on the floor. She led them to the fireplace, where a small hatchet had been placed among the ashes as though it had always belonged there.

The blade was clean. The handle was not.

By dawn, the sun spilled across a crime scene already compromised. A curious crowd had begun to form in the alley. Some came for scandal, others to confirm what they had heard: Helen Jewett—young, beautiful, infamous—was dead.

Helen Jewett was not her real name. But in the candlelit world of Rosina's house, names were flexible. She had arrived two years earlier, a letter of reference in one hand and a well-traveled valise in the other. Tall, arrestingly pale, with eyes the color of green glass, she was different from the other girls. She read voraciously. She wrote letters in long, flowing script. She laughed with clients but rarely revealed anything of herself.

Rosina knew Helen kept secrets. But in that profession, everyone did.

That morning, as the coroner moved through the narrow stairwell and men jostled for a glimpse of the body, Helen's door hung crooked from its hinges. Her mattress was streaked with gore. The police asked who had last seen her alive. One girl, trembling, said she heard a man leave just before the fire. Another claimed to have seen Helen talking to a visitor earlier that evening.

And Rosina? She had her suspicions. A young man named Richard P. Robinson. A law clerk. Educated. Well-dressed. He had been calling on Helen for months. He was a regular, though not always a generous one. The night before, she had seen him come and go.

"Ask him," she told the officers. "Ask Mr. Robinson."

The officers made note, but already they were hesitating. Robinson was not a drunkard. He was not a laborer. He had connections. And the murder of a prostitute, however gruesome, did not always rise to the level of priority for men in uniforms.

But the press was already circling.

By midday, *The Sun* had printed a sensational bulletin. "Beautiful Girl Found Murdered in Brothel!" it read. By nightfall, other papers followed. Rumors spread faster than facts: the door had been locked from the inside; the hatchet belonged to the house; Helen had written letters naming her killer.

Soon, New York was ablaze—not with fire, but with outrage.

She had been just twenty-three. Born Dorcas Doyen in Maine. Orphaned young. Raised by distant relatives. She had worked in respectable homes before turning to sex work—first in Boston, then Providence, then finally New York. She wasn't the only girl to change her name. But few wore theirs with such poise.

Helen walked through parlors like a woman born to velvet. She wrote poetry. She kept a diary. She believed—perhaps foolishly—that the men who came to her bed might one day love her. Or, at the very least, respect her.

That hope ended in blood and ash.

Somewhere in a boardinghouse that same morning, Richard Robinson sat polishing his boots. He claimed to know nothing of the crime. He said he had been home. He said he had left Helen early, hours before the fire. But beneath the calm veneer of his denial, the officers saw something.

Fear.

And so, they brought him in.

She died alone.

No family claimed the body. No procession marked her passing. Her death was brutal, but her silence afterward was worse. The city, so full of noise and progress, paused just long enough to let the blood dry. Then it went on.

But the scars of that night—the screams, the smoke, the stink of burning flesh—remained etched in the memory of the women who worked beside her. They knew it could have been any of them.

They knew that justice, if it came at all, would not come quickly. And it would not come kindly.

Detective's Toolkit

Crime Scene Anomalies in the Pre-Forensic Era (1830s)

- **Locked Room Problem**: The door to Helen's room was reportedly locked from the inside, raising early questions about how the killer exited. This detail remains one of the most perplexing in the case and suggests either staging or misreporting.

- **Murder Weapon**: A small hatchet was found in the fireplace. At the time, fingerprinting was not available, and blood evidence could not be reliably tested, meaning conclusions were drawn almost entirely from circumstantial clues and confessions.

- **Fire as Cover-Up**: The fire was localized, suggesting it was started deliberately—likely intended to obscure evidence of the real cause of death (blunt force trauma).

Fact vs. Speculation Tracker

- **Fact**: Helen Jewett was found dead on April 10, 1836, in a second-story brothel room at 41 Thomas Street.

- **Fact**: The wounds on her head were consistent with blows from a blunt instrument, likely a hatchet.

- **Speculation**: That the fire was meant to destroy evidence or suggest suicide.

- **Speculation**: That Helen had written a letter implicating her killer before her death—no such letter was ever recovered.

Character Spotlight

Rosina Townsend – *Madam of the brothel at 41 Thomas Street*

A woman of survival and sharp instincts, Rosina ran her house with a strict but protective hand. Her business thrived on discretion. The murder shattered that equilibrium. Her early decision to name Richard Robinson as a visitor positioned her both as a witness and a potential liability. In many ways, her life was irrevocably changed the moment she opened Helen's burning door.

Historical Context

New York in 1836: A City of Two Faces

The 1830s marked a time of economic boom and social fragmentation in New York. Wall Street surged ahead while Five Points festered. Brothels thrived in the cracks of moral society, their presence simultaneously condemned and consumed. Police forces were still informal, newspapers were more opinion than record, and women—especially those who lived outside marital norms—had little claim to safety or sympathy in public discourse.

Digital Companion Resources for Chapter 1

- *New York Herald (April 10, 1836)* – Coverage of Helen Jewett's murder scene

- *Rosina Townsend's Court Testimony* – Transcribed excerpts from court records

- *Crime Scenes in 19th-Century New York* – New-York Historical Society archive

- *Helen Jewett: Scandal in the Early Republic* – Patricia Cline Cohen, Yale University Press

Chapter 2:

The Woman on the Bed

At first glance, she looked like a ghost—pale skin glistening with blood and oil, eyes shut as if merely sleeping. The flames had licked the side of her body, leaving patches of her nightdress singed and peeled away. Her head rested at a slight angle, her red hair tangled in ash, the iron frame of the bed casting prison-like shadows across the wall behind her.

But this was no spectral illusion. Helen Jewett was dead, and her death was neither quiet nor clean.

When the fire was doused and the room cleared of smoke, the details began to surface. Her bed was not just scorched—it was soaked through. The mattress had absorbed much of the blood, pooling beneath her head and back. The wound had been deep. A clean, confident blow. Then two more. Not a frenzy, but something calculated.

The hatchet had left crescent-shaped ridges in her skull, severing skin and cracking bone.

A small candle sat half-melted on the side table. Her book lay open beside it, its pages curled from heat but not burned. "The Mysteries of Udolpho." A gothic novel, favored by women who believed romance might still bloom in the margins of danger.

Her slippers were placed neatly at the foot of the bed.

There was no sign of a struggle. No overturned table. No broken glass. The pillow had been pushed aside, not flung. Her inkpot still stood upright. The evidence was cold and precise.

To the officers—and to Rosina, who stood watching with red-rimmed eyes—it did not look like a surprise attack. It looked like a final conversation.

Helen's nightgown had been partially burned, the hem catching fire before it could fully ignite. Her hands were untouched. No defensive wounds. Her body, when lifted slightly, showed no other bruises or abrasions. She had not fought back. Or she had never had the chance.

It was not just the horror of the death that unsettled the watchers. It was the stillness that surrounded it. The stillness of a woman who may have known this end was coming.

Outside the room, life continued. Police constables moved up and down the stairs, asking questions. The other women huddled together in Rosina's parlor, whispering about who might be next. The doctor muttered something about cause of death, but his voice was drowned out by the scraping of the fire grate as someone prodded at the remnants of the hearth.

That's where they found the hatchet.

It was small—compact enough to be concealed beneath a coat. One side of the wooden handle was smeared with something that might have been soot, or might have been blood. The blade had been cleaned, but not polished. There were fibers near the tip. Linen, possibly.

It was not a weapon of impulse. It had been brought to the house.

Whoever had come to Helen's room that night had not come in anger. They had come with intent.

Helen had been beautiful, yes—but that was not what made her remarkable. Many women in brothels were beautiful. What set Helen apart was her poise, her voice, her manner. She moved like a woman who had been educated, trained to hold conversation with men of letters. She quoted poems, debated politics, and chose her clients with the quiet discernment of someone accustomed to navigating power.

She did not beg for affection. She curated it.

Clients who visited her often spoke of her gentleness. Not the kind that submitted, but the kind that listened. Others remembered her sharp wit, her dry observations about their egos and professions. She could be cutting, especially with men who assumed her occupation equated to ignorance. But she was never loud. Never reckless.

She was a study in contradiction.

In death, however, all contradictions were stripped away. The papers did not speak of her as a woman. They spoke of her as a body. They speculated about lovers, grudges, hidden pregnancies. They painted her as a fallen angel— too beautiful, too clever, too ambitious to be allowed to survive.

The word "courtesan" became interchangeable with "murdered."

Her birth name, Dorcas Doyen, vanished from record. The girl who had once walked the forests of Maine, who had read by oil lamp and written long letters to friends in Boston, no longer existed. Helen Jewett had eclipsed her entirely.

Now even Helen was gone.

The coroner arrived late. By then, several reporters had already seen the body. One of them would later describe her in florid detail for the *New York Herald*, noting how her legs were "beautifully formed" and how the bed "bore witness to an act most dreadful."

They did not print her poems. They did not quote her letters.

The doctor made a few notes, observed the wounds, and allowed the body to be removed. No family was notified. No parents stepped forward to claim her.

She was identified only by her employer and her past.

That night, in the house on Thomas Street, Rosina Townsend sat by the fire, watching the shadows move against the wall. She had seen girls come and go. Some left with husbands. Others with children. A few disappeared. One or two died from drink or illness.

But this—this was different.

She lit a second candle. For Helen. For the woman whose real name she had never used, and whose death had now become a spectacle.

She folded a piece of paper, placed it on the mantle, and whispered to no one in particular: "She was better than they said."

She was better than most ever knew.

Detective's Toolkit

Reconstructing the Crime Scene Through Victim Positioning

- **Lack of Struggle**: Helen Jewett's body showed no signs of resistance—suggesting she may have known or trusted her killer, or had been incapacitated quickly.

- **Fire as Concealment**: Arson was likely used to destroy evidence or delay discovery. The fire began on the bed, not near any candle or fireplace—a strong indication of intentional ignition.

- **Weapon Selection**: The hatchet was not a common household object in a brothel. It would have needed to be brought in and hidden, raising questions about premeditation.

Fact vs. Speculation Tracker

- **Fact**: Helen Jewett's body was found in her bed, partially burned, with head trauma from a hatchet.

- **Fact**: The weapon was found in the fireplace, partially cleaned and still embedded with linen fibers.

- **Speculation**: That Helen had been sleeping or sedated before the attack. No toxicology was available to confirm this.

- **Speculation**: That the fire was a spontaneous accident—this is largely ruled out by multiple eyewitnesses and the direction of the burn.

Character Spotlight

Helen Jewett / Dorcas Doyen – *The Victim*

Born in Temple, Maine, around 1813, Helen (née Dorcas) was described as highly literate and strong-willed. After early work as a domestic servant, she turned to sex work—possibly as a form of survival, possibly as reinvention. In

New York, she built a reputation not only for beauty but for intellectual charm. Her death revealed how little society truly valued the complexity of her life.

Historical Context

Women and Respectability in Early 19th-Century America

In the 1830s, women who lived outside marriage or conventional employment were seen as morally suspect. Prostitutes were both tolerated and vilified, existing in a legal gray zone where protection was minimal and violence frequent. The press routinely dehumanized sex workers, treating them as characters in morality tales rather than real people with histories, relationships, and aspirations. Helen's death, and the public reaction to it, is emblematic of the era's intense double standard.

Digital Companion Resources for Chapter 2

- *The New York Herald (April 11, 1836)* – Reporter's description of the crime scene

- *Patricia Cline Cohen, The Murder of Helen Jewett* – Yale University Press

- *Coroner's Findings in the Case of Helen Jewett* – Transcribed archival excerpts

- *American Brothels in the 1830s* – New-York Historical Society documentation

- *Letters and Writings Attributed to Helen Jewett* – Selected pieces from court evidence

Chapter 3:

Rosina Townsend's House

From the street, 41 Thomas Street gave no hint of scandal. A modest three-story brick building, it sat among merchant shops and oyster houses, its blinds drawn tight and its steps swept clean. No music wafted from its windows. No painted women leaned out from balconies. This was not the bawdy chaos of the Bowery. This was discretion, discipline—Rosina Townsend's signature.

Inside, the house was hushed. Not lifeless, but orderly. A place where the women did not shriek or drink to excess, where clients were reminded they were visitors, not masters. The velvet settee in the parlor was kept free of stains. The clocks were wound nightly. Towels were boiled in vinegar water and changed after every appointment. Rosina tolerated indulgence—but never disorder.

That morning, even with the blood still soaking through Helen's mattress and smoke clinging to the upstairs walls, Rosina's first act was to check the ledgers.

Two girls had already left. Another packed her things in silence, face pale, eyes trained on her own door. They had come here for protection as much as profit. And now one of them was gone—not from escape, but from violence.

Rosina stood at the foot of the staircase, her fingers wrapped tightly around the rail. She had run this house for nearly eight years. Before that, a smaller one in Chatham Square. Before that, she worked for others—learning which clients tipped in coins and which in bruises. She was not soft, but she was fair. Her reputation, like her establishment, was built brick by brick.

She had known Helen would not last forever. Beauty like that invited danger. But she had not expected it this soon, or this brutal.

She climbed the stairs slowly, her heels clicking against the grain of the wood. On the second floor, the hallway held its breath. Helen's room, now a charred shrine, had been sealed by police with a scrap of cloth tied to the doorknob. The other girls' doors were shut, locked from within. Even the gaslights seemed dimmer.

The parlor, by contrast, still held its sense of performance. The rug was plush, though faded. A portrait of a young woman in empire dress hung above the fireplace—a reminder of an era when this kind of house might have served more refined patrons. A piano sat silent in the corner. Rosina's ledger lay open on the writing desk, filled with initials and appointment times, coded to mean everything and nothing.

Beneath it was Helen's note from three nights ago. Neat script. A request for a later supper. Nothing ominous. Nothing fearful.

A knock at the door made her flinch.

It was a constable—again. Another round of questions. Had Helen argued with anyone? Had any gentleman behaved oddly? Had any girls mentioned jealousy or threats?

Rosina answered each query with the precision of a woman who had memorized her lines. She did not speculate. She did not guess. She reported only what she could swear to. And when asked if Helen had recently entertained a man named Robinson, she paused.

"Yes," she said at last. "Several times."

They had come and gone through the front entrance, like any other guests. No cloaks or disguises. No aliases—at least none given to her. Just quiet, pale-faced men with pockets full of coin and too much loneliness to keep it.

That was the nature of this house. It was a mirror. And everyone who stepped inside saw only what they wanted to.

In the back room, where Rosina kept her books and correspondence, there was a drawer she had not yet opened. It held the letters Helen had entrusted her with months before. "If anything happens," she'd said, not laughing, not even smiling. "Don't read them. But don't throw them out either."

Rosina unlocked the drawer.

Inside, tied with a faded ribbon, were three envelopes. All sealed. All addressed to the same man.

She closed the drawer again.

Detective's Toolkit

Understanding the Function of a Discreet Brothel in 1830s Manhattan

- **Client Logs and Pseudonyms**: Brothels often kept coded ledgers, recording clients by initials or symbols to protect their identities. These records were rarely admissible in court due to lack of full names or corroborating witnesses.

- **Social Duality**: While officially outlawed, many such houses operated with quiet permission from local authorities—particularly when frequented by men of standing. Rosina's brothel maintained such equilibrium: invisible to reformers, tolerated by police, and patronized by clerks, lawyers, and even politicians.

Fact vs. Speculation Tracker

- **Fact**: 41 Thomas Street was owned and operated by Rosina Townsend, who managed a quiet, orderly brothel with a small circle of girls.

- **Fact**: Helen Jewett resided there for several months prior to her murder and was seen frequently with Richard P. Robinson.

- **Speculation**: That Helen had expressed fear or suspicion in her final days. No letter or testimony directly confirmed this at the time.

- **Speculation**: That Rosina withheld evidence—particularly letters—from police. This remains unconfirmed.

Character Spotlight

Rosina Townsend – *Madam, Witness, Survivor*

Rosina ran her house like a business—one that depended on discretion, routine, and strict boundaries. In a society that offered little protection for women in her trade, Rosina created a haven with rules. Her testimony at Robinson's trial was direct and unwavering. Some painted her as complicit; others as the only voice brave enough to speak truth in a room full of fear. Either way, she outlived the scandal—but not the shame attached to it.

Historical Context

The Politics of Prostitution in 1830s New York

In antebellum Manhattan, brothels like Rosina's were both omnipresent and unspeakable. Reformers fought to shut them down, while city officials quietly profited from their existence. Women who ran such houses were caught in a paradox: criminalized by law, but relied upon for social balance. Respectable men visited these homes by night and condemned them by day. Public exposure of a house like 41 Thomas Street often meant ruin—not just for the madam, but for the entire community of women who lived inside.

Digital Companion Resources for Chapter 3

- *New York Evening Post (April 1836)* – Coverage of Rosina Townsend's testimony

- *Court Transcript: People v. Robinson, 1836* – Rosina's statements to investigators

- *Historical Records of Brothels in Early Manhattan* – New York Public Library Archives

- *Cline Cohen, Patricia – The Murder of Helen Jewett* – Chapters 3–5: Townsend's background and house rules

- *Map of Thomas Street, 1836* – NY Historical Society: Lower Manhattan cartography archive

Chapter 4:

Locked From the Inside

The room no longer smelled of perfume.

By the time investigators pushed open the scorched door to Helen Jewett's chamber, the fire had long since smothered itself into ash. A sooty crust clung to the wallpaper above the bed, and the heavy curtains had melted into blackened cords. Smoke still lingered faintly in the air—a bitter residue of violence—and the floorboards beneath the mattress were slick with congealed blood.

Lieutenant George W. Matsell stepped cautiously over the threshold, handkerchief pressed to his mouth. He had seen knife fights, wharf shootings, and drownings pulled from the East River. But this—this was different. The brutality was personal. Focused. It wasn't rage in a moment. It was intention.

The bed was the centerpiece. A low, carved walnut frame with a canopy scorched from flame. Helen's body had been found half-naked, her nightgown soaked in blood, her head caved in with what must have been a small, heavy blade—likely a hatchet. The pillow was cut clean through. There was no struggle on the floor. No sign of a chase. She had not screamed loud enough for anyone to hear—or perhaps she had been silenced too quickly.

And then there was the door.

Latched from the inside.

It was Rosina Townsend who first told them. "I had to break in," she said. "The door wouldn't budge."

She had used a spare key—but the bolt, slid from the inside, had made the frame swell. A sharp shoulder to the wood finally gave way. By then, the smoke was curling through the hallway, and the bed was glowing orange.

That lock puzzled everyone.

Whoever had killed Helen, lit the fire, and fled—had done so without leaving through that door.

Or they never left at all.

Matsell examined the windows. Both were closed, shutters latched. One was slightly loose on its hinge, but there were no footprints in the flower box beneath. No broken glass. No scuff on the sill.

The girls downstairs hadn't heard anyone leave.

The backyard was enclosed. No one reported a shadow crossing it that night.

And then there was the hatchet.

It had been left behind. Propped against the wall, as if placed—rather than dropped. Its blade was slick with blood, the handle wiped clean. Too clean.

Matsell retrieved it with a gloved hand and bagged it. It would be the centerpiece of the coming trial. But even now, he sensed it might not be enough.

He turned to the writing desk. Helen's comb was there, still twined with strands of auburn hair. A broken quill. A blotter soaked in ink. Letters—some open, some torn. One bore a familiar name: *R.P.R.*

That name would unravel everything.

As more officers poured into the room, questions formed like fog:

Why lock the door from the inside?

Was the fire a panic? Or a calculated attempt to erase evidence?

What kind of man carries a hatchet to a woman's bed—and leaves it behind?

Matsell looked once more at the pillow, cleaved in two.

There had been no mercy in this room.

Only precision.

Only silence.

Only Helen.

Detective's Toolkit

The Locked Room Problem in 1830s Forensics

- **Interior Bolting**: In 1836, a room bolted from the inside suggested suicide—or clever deception. Without modern latches or reverse locks, investigators debated whether the killer escaped before locking the door, or used sleight of hand to trick the bolt shut from outside.

- **Arson as Evidence Tampering**: Fire destroys evidence, but it also creates clues. The direction of the burn, origin point, and state of furnishings all helped investigators determine whether a blaze was staged. In Helen's case, the fire began at the foot of the bed—on her chemise.

Fact vs. Speculation Tracker

- **Fact**: Helen Jewett's door was locked from the inside. Rosina had to break in.

- **Fact**: A hatchet with blood residue was found at the scene, partially wiped clean.

- **Fact**: The fire originated from Helen's bedclothes, not from an accidental source.

- **Speculation**: The killer escaped through a secret passage or secondary door. No such exit has ever been confirmed.

- **Speculation**: Helen may have known her killer and let them in willingly—implied by lack of forced entry.

Character Spotlight

Lieutenant George Washington Matsell – *Early Forensic Thinker in a City of Smoke*

Later to become New York's first Police Commissioner, Matsell was one of the few officers in the 1830s who treated crime scenes with deliberation. Though limited by the tools of his era, his careful documentation of Helen's room and his interrogation of witnesses would set precedents in American investigative practice. He was also a keen observer of social class and suspected—quietly—that Robinson's money and position might bend the arc of justice.

Historical Context

Urban Crime Scene Management in Pre-Modern Policing

The New York police force in the 1830s was still more of a loose assembly than a formal institution. There was no fingerprinting, no blood typing, and certainly no crime labs. Crime scenes were quickly contaminated, often overrun by journalists or neighbors. The idea of preserving evidence was radical—almost absurd. Yet the Helen Jewett case prompted a shift, as both public outrage and police embarrassment fueled early reforms in how murders were documented and tried.

Digital Companion Resources for Chapter 4

- *New York Herald (April 11, 1836)* – Original reporting on the locked door and fire

- *Trial Transcripts of People v. Robinson* – Evidence logs from the scene

- *Historical NYC Crime Scene Reconstruction Techniques* – NYPD Archive Retrospective

- *The Murder of Helen Jewett by Patricia Cline Cohen* – Chapter 6: The Locked Room Puzzle

- *Map of Thomas Street, 1830s* – New York Historical Society Cartography Division

PART II –

Lives That Led to Death

In the quiet aftermath of a murder, time does not simply resume—it distorts. Whispers replace voices. Judgments take root. And in 1836, after the flames at 41 Thomas Street had been extinguished and Helen Jewett's body removed, a different kind of heat began to smolder: the fire of speculation. Before justice could even reach for her, society had already begun to revise her. To dismember her identity not with hatchets, but with headlines.

This part of the story does not begin with blood, but with *before*. Before she was the girl in the papers. Before she was reduced to the phrase "fallen woman." Before the locked door, the hatchet, the silk nightgown drenched in flame. This is where we peel back the aliases and assumptions, and meet the lives that led to Helen Jewett's death.

Her name, first of all, was not Helen. She had been born **Dorcas Doyen**—a bright, stubborn girl raised in the forests of Maine, surrounded by piety and poverty. Her father's death cast a long shadow across her adolescence. From those roots of loss and reinvention sprang a young woman both admired and feared: intelligent beyond her years, unnervingly self-possessed, and determined never to live at the mercy of another man again.

As Dorcas grew into Helen, she mastered the art of transformation. But every mask she donned was welded from necessity. She learned to control the gaze of men— then to profit from it. Moving from house to house, lover to lover, she elevated herself from mere prostitute to **courtesan**—an uncommon distinction in early 19th-century New York. She wore velvet and feathers, smoked cigars, and read novels considered too risqué for women of her class. She was bold in a city that demanded submission. And for that, she became both object of desire and symbol of transgression.

But Helen was not alone in her double life.

In another part of the city, a young clerk was rising in a respectable law office. He signed his name as **Richard P. Robinson**, but in secret letters to Helen, he called himself

"Frank Rivers." Handsome, socially connected, and just nineteen years old, Robinson played at mystery even as he attended tea with judges and walked the avenues with the sons of merchants. His nights, however, led him to brothels—especially Rosina Townsend's house, where Helen resided. What he sought there wasn't just sex. It was *control*. To be known without consequences. To be powerful without responsibility.

Their affair spanned months, maybe longer. In public, he denied her. In private, he confided to her. Helen kept letters—some romantic, some threatening. She sensed instability in him. He, in turn, began to feel the precarious edge of her knowledge.

Meanwhile, a circle of men drifted through Helen's orbit. Clients. Patrons. Threats. Some left quietly with money and secrets intact. Others returned with jealous fury, driven by the toxic blend of possession and shame. Among them: a man who called himself "Mr. Tew," another who used the name "Bill Easy." What they had in common was access. What they lacked was consequence.

This part of the book reconstructs the week before Helen's murder—not through official timelines, but through **personal letters, conflicting testimonies, and fragmented truths**. We watch her write her final journal entries. We trace Robinson's coded correspondences. We see the contours of a powder keg taking shape—volatile emotions cloaked in civility, whispered threats behind closed doors.

These chapters do not merely offer backstory. They set the stage for betrayal. Because Helen's murder was not a spontaneous act. It was **an ending scripted by many hands**—by a city that punished the women it exploited, by a man whose image could not withstand exposure, and by a system that viewed sex as a crime only when the woman survived to speak of it.

Here, reputations become weapons. Here, we witness how the choices of the living paved the path toward the death of a woman whose greatest crime was trying to control her own story.

And as the trial looms, the stakes rise—not only for Robinson, but for every woman in Rosina's house. Their safety, their identities, and their futures become collateral in the fight for narrative dominance. Was Helen a scorned lover or a calculating seductress? Was Robinson a sociopathic killer or the victim of a scandalous frame-up?

Part II invites readers to **examine the intimate machinery behind the crime**. It is not just a history of Helen and Richard—it is a diagnosis of a culture that blurred consent and coercion, privilege and immunity.

Before the courtroom. Before the headlines.

There was *them*.

And everything that went unsaid.

Chapter 5:

Helen Jewett Wasn't Always Helen

The girl who would die as Helen Jewett was born under another name—**Dorcas Doyen**, a name better suited for a Puritan gravestone than a city brothel. Her life began in **Temple, Maine**, around 1813, nestled in the timbered hills and snow-fed streams of Franklin County. In a village where horses outnumbered books and winters taught endurance, the transformation from a child of the woods to a courtesan in New York City required not just strength, but *imagination*. Dorcas possessed both.

Her father, **George Doyen**, was a working-class man with aspirations that exceeded his means. He died when Dorcas was still a girl—some say from illness, others from the quiet despair that claimed many men of his station. His absence carved a void in the family structure, leaving Dorcas to navigate the world with her mother, who would remarry a man described as stern and unyielding. The new household was not unkind, but it was brittle. And Dorcas, brilliant and restless, grew to resent its narrow confines.

Early accounts suggest she was a **precocious student**. She devoured books when she could find them. A neighbor recalled her as "sharp-tongued and light on her feet," while a childhood tutor noted, "She had a strange way of looking straight through you—as if already weighing your usefulness." Her penmanship was elegant, her grammar precise. She was, by all accounts, not merely literate—but *literary*.

By her early teens, she had secured a position as a **servant in the home of Judge Weston**, a respected jurist in Augusta, Maine. The judge's house was unlike anything she had known—books in every room, arguments over law and politics at the table, men of influence constantly passing through the front parlor. Dorcas watched, learned, and listened. She also, by rumor, seduced.

When the judge's wife dismissed her abruptly, the whispers followed: that Dorcas had become too familiar with the judge. That letters were exchanged. That she had developed a dangerous sense of power. Whether true or not, her sudden departure from the Weston home marked the end of her rural respectability.

By 16, she was in **Portland**, then **Boston**, and soon **New York**—reinventing herself each time. Dorcas Doyen became Helen Jewett, a name that rolled easily off the tongue, as crisp as the silk she would later wear in Rosina Townsend's parlor. She was no longer the girl from Maine. She was now *someone else entirely*.

Helen was not like the other women in the brothels. She spoke in measured tones, read novels aloud to her clients, and wrote letters that sometimes felt more like essays. She could quote Byron and discuss tariffs. She was beautiful, yes—dark curls, grey eyes, and a mouth shaped like something half-daring, half-tired—but what made her dangerous was not her body. It was her mind.

In a letter to a friend in Boston, she once wrote: **"Men desire mystery, so I become a cipher they must pay to solve. But when they learn the answer, they wish they hadn't."**

— Letter attributed to Helen Jewett, private collection, 1835

She curated her image. Helen styled herself in velvet and plum-colored silks, wrapped her hair in peacock-colored scarves, and even had calling cards embossed with her name. She was a courtesan in the French tradition—less streetwalker, more *muse*. She cultivated a clientele of literate, often powerful men. Some were mesmerized. Others were terrified.

Still, the lines between safety and performance blurred.

Despite her control, Helen was never entirely safe. She lived on the margins—**too educated to be dismissed, too defiant to be owned**. Her letters became a form of protection—evidence, bargaining chips, or perhaps confessions. Some were written in affection, others in anger. A few, in fear.

By 1835, she had begun seeing **Richard P. Robinson**, a young clerk in a respected law firm. Their relationship, if one could call it that, was inconsistent—full of flirtation, jealousy, and volatility. She referred to him alternately as

"Frank Rivers" and "that devil of a boy." He, in turn, wrote her notes that oscillated between infatuation and threats. Some clients Helen kept for money. Others, for information. Robinson may have been both.

Helen's identity was both shield and weapon. She was **a woman forged in contradiction**: a victim of economic desperation who mastered the market she was born to be devoured by. She sold companionship, but often sought sincerity. She navigated male egos like an actress moving between roles. And she knew too well the price of slipping out of character.

Still, even Helen could not control everything. In the weeks before her death, friends noted she had grown tense. She had argued with Rosina. She was seen pacing, writing furiously, burning letters in the hearth. Whether she feared Robinson, or something else entirely, remains uncertain.

She had built herself from ash. But the fire was coming again.

Character Spotlight

Dorcas Doyen / Helen Jewett – Born into obscurity and raised in discipline, Dorcas transformed herself into Helen Jewett, a woman of words, wit, and calculated allure. Her life was a study in performance, ambition, and risk—a girl who refused to be ordinary, and who paid the price for living on her own terms.

Historical Context

In early 19th-century America, opportunities for women were brutally limited. For working-class girls like Dorcas Doyen, options often included domestic service, factory labor, or sex work. Brothels, especially high-end ones like Rosina Townsend's, offered a paradox: degradation and income, danger and independence. A literate courtesan was both fascinating and threatening. Helen's attempt to balance autonomy and survival placed her in constant peril—socially, legally, and emotionally.

Fact vs. Speculation Tracker

- **Fact:** Helen Jewett was born Dorcas Doyen in Temple, Maine, around 1813.

- **Fact:** She worked in the home of Judge Weston before being dismissed under unclear circumstances.

- **Speculation:** Helen had an affair with the judge, leading to her removal from the household.

- **Speculation:** She maintained blackmail material on her clients, including letters. No such material was recovered from the crime scene.

- **Fact:** Helen was using the name "Helen Jewett" by the time she arrived in New York and established herself as a courtesan.

Detective's Toolkit

Alias Use and Identity in 19th-Century Sex Work

- Women in brothels often adopted aliases to protect themselves from social ruin. These names also allowed them to rebuild their reputations when changing cities or houses.

- Helen's use of aliases—especially "Helen Jewett"— was strategic, allowing her to reinvent herself while concealing her past.

- Identity theft, false references, and pseudonyms were common tools for women navigating the double standards of morality and survival.

Digital Companion Resources for Chapter 5

Temple, Maine Historical Census Records – Maine State Archives

Private Letters Attributed to Helen Jewett (Dorcas Doyen) – Harvard University, Houghton Library

New York Courtesans and the 1830s Vice Economy – JSTOR Journal Article

Weston Family Correspondence (1820s–30s) – Maine Historical Society

Early American Sex Work Laws and Social Norms –
Library of Congress Archive

Chapter 6:

The Clerk Who Called Himself Rivers

The boy who became Helen Jewett's final companion in life and first suspect in her death entered New York not as a criminal—but as a rising star in a suit. **Richard P. Robinson**, barely twenty years old, was the kind of young man clerks admired and bank directors tolerated. With his fine handwriting, calm demeanor, and steady ascent through the merchant class, he looked every inch the self-made success story that early 19th-century America liked to believe in.

But like Helen, Richard lived behind masks. And one of them was signed, *Frank Rivers*.

He'd arrived in the city from Connecticut, the product of a modest but respectable family—his father a shoemaker, his siblings scattered through respectable trades. His letters bore the hallmarks of someone well-educated, if not deeply thoughtful. In public, he was quiet, refined, and liked to be seen as above scandal. But in private—especially at night—he frequented places his daytime self pretended not to know existed.

Robinson worked at the firm **Phoenix and Alsop**, a well-known merchant house on Maiden Lane. It was said he was efficient, punctual, and aloof—never quite warm, but never openly cruel. He spent his evenings not in saloons but in parlors, gambling rooms, and brothels. He played the piano when asked. He took his tea cold. He wrote long letters in a delicate script, folding them with precise corners and sealing them in green wax. Helen kept many of them.

One, found after her death, read:

"You insist upon troubling me again, though I have given you reason not to. I must again request that you refrain. You know what I mean."

— Letter from Richard Robinson to Helen Jewett, March 1836

He sometimes denied he was the author. But the handwriting was unmistakably his.

Among the women at Rosina Townsend's house, Robinson was known as a **cold flirt**, a man who liked control but rarely revealed his own desires. He courted Helen not with passion, but with possession. Witnesses later said he became jealous of her other clients, though he refused to call her his mistress. When she confronted him—allegedly about letters or gossip or threats—he withdrew. And when he returned, something had shifted.

By early 1836, Helen had confided in Rosina that she feared "trouble with Rivers." There were threats—not overt, but implied. She told one of the other girls, "If anything happens to me, you know who." When asked why she didn't report it, she laughed. "And say what? That a clerk threatened me with silence?"

Character Spotlight

Richard P. Robinson – Intelligent, composed, and socially ambitious, Robinson embodied the contradictions of his class: moral in posture, reckless in shadow. His double life—law clerk by day, brothel patron by night— mirrored the Victorian tension between respectability and desire. Helen was drawn to him not despite these contradictions, but perhaps because of them.

On the night of April 9, 1836, Robinson arrived at 41 Thomas Street under the name *Frank Rivers*. He was seen by **Rosina Townsend** and others around 9 p.m. He asked for Helen. She was in the front room, already dressed for the evening. He paid for her time and followed her upstairs. Hours later, she would be dead.

Rosina would later recall how calm he seemed. "Polite. More so than usual. And quiet." He had a cloak, dark and broad-shouldered, and his boots were unusually clean. He left around 1 a.m., according to one witness. Another girl thought she heard footsteps just after midnight. A third said she thought she smelled smoke.

The next morning, after the horror was discovered and the police alerted, **Richard Robinson was arrested at his boarding house** on Cedar Street. He protested. He insisted he had been reading at home. But his demeanor betrayed something: not panic, but irritation. When told

Helen had been murdered, he replied: "So help me God, I am innocent."

Police searched his quarters. They found a **cloak**, freshly laundered, drying by the fire. A hatchet, believed to be the murder weapon, had been taken from the scene but showed no fingerprints—an unremarkable fact in a world before fingerprinting was common practice. Witnesses disagreed on when they saw him leave. Some said he slipped out quietly; others weren't sure he left at all.

His trial would soon become one of the first *media-fueled moral battlegrounds* in American legal history. But in the hours after his arrest, Richard Robinson was just a boy in a room, trembling in linen, clinging to a story that shifted depending on who asked.

Detective's Toolkit

Alias Use in Urban Crime Networks

- The use of aliases like "Frank Rivers" allowed young men of means to separate their social standing from their nocturnal habits. In the 1830s, this practice was widespread among lawyers, clerks, and politicians.

- Aliases served both as disguise and plausible deniability. For someone like Robinson, it wasn't just about deception—it was about *compartmentalization*.

Fact vs. Speculation Tracker

- **Fact:** Richard Robinson was arrested on April 10, 1836, the morning after Helen's murder.

- **Fact:** He had used the alias "Frank Rivers" at brothels, including Rosina Townsend's.

- **Speculation:** Robinson threatened Helen in writing; no letter explicitly threatening her life was confirmed.

- **Fact:** A cloak linked to Robinson was found drying in his room after the murder.

- **Speculation:** The cloak had bloodstains that were cleaned; testing was inconclusive by 1836 standards.

- **Fact:** Robinson denied the murder, claiming he was reading at home, alone.

Historical Context

In 1830s New York, the **merchant class** was exploding. Clerks like Robinson were the new aspirants—men who didn't inherit wealth but hoped to earn it through discretion, loyalty, and networked ambition. Reputation was everything. A scandal could end a career before it began. For such men, women like Helen were not merely company—they were risk.

Digital Companion Resources for Chapter 6

New York Merchant Clerks and Social Ambition – Gilder Lehrman Institute

Robinson's Letter to Helen Jewett (Original Manuscript) – New-York Historical Society

Phoenix and Alsop Company Records, Maiden Lane – NYU Archives

Alias Use and Sex Work in Antebellum New York – Columbia Law Review

Arrest Report of Richard Robinson, April 10, 1836 – The Sun Archive

Chapter 7:

Between Clients and Confessions

The days before Helen Jewett's death were filled with routine—if the routines of a sex worker in 1830s New York could ever be called ordinary. There were letters written and received, appointments made and broken, familiar faces welcomed upstairs, and others turned away. But something in the rhythm of her final week was off, as if she sensed something darker taking shape behind the curtains of her rented room.

She had taken to writing more in her journal. The pages, filled with neat, practiced script, oscillated between weariness and defiance. Her tone suggested a woman accustomed to secrecy but no longer comforted by it. In one entry, dated just days before her death, she wrote:

"I have been warned again not to provoke him. But what is left to lose when one's virtue is already public property?" — *Recovered Journal Entry, April 1836*

The "him" was never named. But those who knew her best believed it to be Richard Robinson. And Helen, no stranger to danger, seemed unusually on edge in the final days of her life. Rosina Townsend later testified that Helen had become withdrawn, but not fearful—just watchful. "She carried herself like she was waiting for something to happen," Rosina told police. "Or someone."

Witnesses would later piece together the fragments of Helen's final week. She had received a letter from a client—possibly Robinson—though its contents were never made public. She entertained her usual callers, including a man known only as *Mr. Tew*, who often brought her imported cigarettes and spoke to her of Paris. Another frequent visitor, referred to in surviving records as *Bill Easy*, was reportedly seen arguing with her on the street the Wednesday before her death.

A washerwoman employed by Rosina claimed she saw Helen "tear up a letter in anger" two nights before the murder. Another girl in the house remembered her sitting by the hearth long after midnight, staring into the coals. "She wasn't crying," the girl said, "but she looked...

disappointed. Like the kind of disappointment that only comes when you realize someone you trusted isn't coming back."

On April 9, Helen prepared her room as she always did—tidying the washbasin, adjusting the silk screen by her bed, and placing her rosewood hairbrush on the small table beneath the mirror. She lit a single candle, trimmed the wick to avoid sputtering, and waited.

Richard Robinson arrived just past nine o'clock, using his alias: *Frank Rivers*. Rosina greeted him. He was wearing gloves. He asked directly for Helen.

According to Rosina's later testimony:

"She seemed stiff when she opened the door for him. She smiled, but it didn't reach her eyes. I remember because I thought to myself—something's changed between them."

What happened between 9 p.m. and the time of the fire is known only through reconstruction. No one heard screams. No thudding footsteps. No shattered glass. Just the soft groan of a stairboard as someone descended long after midnight, and the flicker of flame seen too late.

Emotional Anchor

Helen's final letter, found half-written in her belongings, was addressed not to a lover, but to her sister in Maine. She never finished it. The last line read:

"I have made peace with the world, though I doubt it has done the same for me."

It is a chilling reminder that Helen, who reinvented herself from Dorcas Doyen to Helen Jewett, lived a life suspended between defiance and desperation—always watching the door, always writing to someone who might never write back.

Detective's Toolkit

Reading Victim Behavior in the Final Days

- Modern investigators often look at changes in a victim's routine or temperament in the days leading up to a violent crime.

- Helen's shift—from open conversation to quiet watchfulness—may suggest foreknowledge or dread.

- The torn letter, noted by a servant, could be vital. In contemporary investigations, discarded correspondence can reveal threats or blackmail motives.

Fact vs. Speculation Tracker

- **Fact:** Helen met with multiple clients in the days before her death.

- **Fact:** Richard Robinson sent at least one letter to Helen shortly before her murder.

- **Speculation:** The torn letter recovered was from Robinson—its authorship remains unproven.

- **Fact:** Helen was seen behaving unusually the night before her death—quiet, introspective.

- **Speculation:** Helen believed her life was in danger—no direct evidence confirms this fear.

Character Spotlight

"Bill Easy" and "Mr. Tew" – These were aliases or nicknames for regular clients of Helen's. While both had alibis during the time of the murder, they represent the gray fog surrounding Helen's world: men with influence, concealed identities, and complicated affections. In many ways, they were reflections of the city itself—charming by day, dangerous by night.

Historical Context

In 1830s New York, brothels were more than dens of vice— they were embedded in the city's social and political network. Many men who visited Rosina's house were clerks, lawyers, and minor officials. Their identities were guarded by custom and coin, and women like Helen were expected to maintain that silence. Breaking it—through gossip, letters, or accusation—was seen as betrayal. Punishable betrayal.

Digital Companion Resources for Chapter 7

Helen Jewett's Journal Fragments – New-York Historical Society Archive

Rosina Townsend Police Statement (April 10, 1836) – The Sun Archive

Profile of Clients in 1830s Manhattan Brothels – Journal of American Urban History

Alias Records from Thomas Street Brothels – Columbia University Case Database

Contemporary Map of Thomas Street and Surroundings – David Rumsey Map Collection

---

Chapter 8:

The Circle of Men

The rooms of 41 Thomas Street were never truly quiet. Even in the hours before dawn, boots could be heard on the stairs, the rustle of coats, the hiss of whispered names, and the low, careful click of doors closing behind men who didn't wish to be seen. The house, though legally described as a boarding establishment, functioned like many of its kind: a discreet theater of vice patronized by gentlemen in need of release—and in need of silence.

Helen Jewett's clientele, like the women who worked beside her, were part of a secret city that operated parallel to the polite one. Men from law offices, shipping firms, and countinghouses. Men whose names appeared in ledgers by day and were spoken only in aliases by night.

On paper, Helen's address book was modest. But beneath the ink were aliases and codes—"T.R.," "Mr. Tew," "Easy Bill," "the one from Wall Street"—names that seemed designed to protect not just identities, but reputations. Some of these men left behind letters. Others left behind only rumor. A few, like Richard Robinson, left behind a question: how far would a man go to silence a woman who knew him too well?

One of the first names to emerge during the investigation was *Mr. Tew*. Described by multiple witnesses as a "gentleman of refined habits," Tew was rumored to be involved in politics or publishing. He often visited Helen late at night, sometimes staying until dawn. He brought imported cigars, spoke of Paris, and once promised to send her to Europe. According to Rosina, Helen found him "charming but dangerous in his quiet way."

Then there was *Bill Easy*, a far rougher presence—taller, louder, and prone to outbursts. A former dockworker turned low-level enforcer for a shipping firm, Bill Easy had reportedly quarreled with Helen twice in the week leading up to her death. On one occasion, he was seen grabbing her arm on Broadway and whispering something that made her go pale.

A third man, whose name is never recorded, was identified only as "the boy with the ink-stained cuffs." He had visited Helen several times in March, each time bringing her flowers and an envelope of money. Some suspected he worked in Robinson's law office. Others claimed he was a decoy—someone sent by Robinson to keep tabs on Helen when their relationship soured.

By the time of the murder, Helen's interactions with her clients had begun to shift. She had spoken to at least two women in the house about leaving the profession. According to one, she had "a plan"—though whether that plan involved blackmail, marriage, or escape remains unclear. But what is certain is that several of her former clients had reason to be nervous.

When detectives began asking questions in the aftermath of the murder, many of these men vanished. A few sent letters of condolence to Rosina, all unsigned. One sent money for a burial plot. None offered testimony. The brothel's visitor records, if they existed, were either destroyed or never kept at all. And Rosina, fearing for her own safety, quickly adopted a code of silence when it came to identifying anyone with political or economic power.

Emotional Anchor

Helen's world was shaped by the men who passed through it—some who adored her, some who exploited her, many who feared her. In the end, it may have been fear—not love, not hate—that killed her. Fear of exposure. Fear of scandal. Fear that the woman lying in bed could speak too clearly of what had passed behind closed doors.

Detective's Toolkit

Client Lists and Alias Codes in Historical Vice Investigations

- In 19th-century brothels, women often kept coded logs of their clients for safety and leverage.

- Names were abbreviated, real identities rarely written. This protected clients but made post-crime investigations nearly impossible.

- In modern criminal investigations, such lists—if recovered—can be forensically cross-referenced with handwriting analysis, financial records, or call logs. In Helen's time, no such tools were available.

Fact vs. Speculation Tracker

- **Fact:** Helen had multiple regular clients, some of whom visited her in the final days before her death.

- **Fact:** Witnesses confirmed quarrels with at least one client, "Bill Easy."

- **Speculation:** "Mr. Tew" was politically connected—his identity was never confirmed.

- **Fact:** Helen had expressed a desire to leave the brothel and begin a new life.

- **Speculation:** She may have been preparing to expose or blackmail a former client.

Character Spotlight

Rosina Townsend – The madam who knew everything but said very little. Rosina's testimony to police was measured and strategic. She protected the living more than the dead. Her decision not to expose certain clients likely saved her from legal reprisal—and possibly from further violence.

Historical Context

In the early 19th century, sex work existed in a legal and moral gray zone. The men who used it were protected by social codes of discretion. The women who provided it were seen as fallen, disposable. When crimes occurred in these spaces, justice bent to the reputations of the powerful. Brothel murders were often unsolved not because they were mysteries, but because too many people wanted them to remain so.

Digital Companion Resources for Chapter 8

Reconstructed Client Alias Logs from 1830s Brothels – New-York Historical Society

Rosina Townsend's Post-Trial Interviews – The Sun Archive, 1836

Profile of Vice and Class in Antebellum New York – NYU Urban History Research

Newspaper Illustration of "Bill Easy" Alleged Confrontation – The Morning Courier

Map of Lower Manhattan Vice Districts (1830–1840) – Library of Congress Collection

---

PART III –

Trial by Reputation

Focus: The legal unraveling, press manipulation, and gendered courtroom warfare

The courtroom was not just a space for law—it was a stage. And in the case of Helen Jewett, the trial of Richard P. Robinson became a full-blown theater of character assassination, class warfare, and journalistic spectacle. Part III of this book delves into the high drama that unfolded in the wake of Helen's murder, when justice was not only sought but performed.

By the summer of 1836, the city of New York had already been consumed by the story. Helen's murder had ignited not just a criminal inquiry, but a moral panic. Who was this woman, really? A victim or a seductress? And what of the man accused—young, educated, ambitious Richard Robinson? The public didn't just want justice; they wanted a narrative that affirmed their fears or soothed their discomfort. And for the media, that hunger became an opportunity.

James Gordon Bennett, a scrappy Scottish immigrant and editor of the fledgling *New York Herald*, seized this moment. His vivid reporting—often bending the line between fact and fiction—gave Helen's death a new life in print. The brothel became an emblem of urban corruption. Robinson a symbol of fallen privilege. And Rosina Townsend, the madam who dared to speak, a lightning rod of scorn or sympathy depending on who held the pen.

This part of the book examines how the trial unfolded not simply in the courtroom, but in the pages of the newspapers and in the whispered gossip of parlors and saloons. It asks: how was Helen's morality used as a defense for her own killer? How did the press bend reality to protect men like Robinson—and what did they gain from it?

Inside the courtroom, it was not a question of forensic evidence. That was thin. Instead, the focus became personal testimony, perceived virtue, and class alignment. Ogden Hoffman, Robinson's skilled defense attorney, crafted a case that didn't just dispute facts—it dismantled Helen's credibility as a human being. Rosina was painted as opportunistic. The other girls in the house? Dismissed as liars or worse.

This was a trial that weaponized womanhood. Helen was not afforded the dignity of innocence. Her murder was treated as an inevitability—perhaps even deserved. Meanwhile, Robinson's supporters flooded the gallery. Their murmurs of approval during cross-examinations were not just audible—they were sanctioned by a society eager to restore balance by dismissing the disruption that Helen's murder had caused.

Despite key testimony, including from Rosina and the circumstantial discovery of Robinson's cloak, the tide turned against justice. The prosecution failed to present a coherent motive. The jury, composed of men of similar social class to Robinson, took only fifteen minutes to reach their verdict. It was not guilt. It was relief.

This section also documents the role of early criminal defense strategy in America. The Robinson case set precedents not in law, but in public manipulation. It showed how character defense—especially in cases involving sex work—could completely override forensic detail. It exposed the growing chasm between morality and justice in American courts.

Part III is where the tragedy curdles into farce. Where Helen, already brutalized in life and death, is obliterated anew by language, bias, and performance. And where Robinson—guilty or not—becomes less a man on trial and more a symbol of privilege defended at all costs.

But beyond the verdict, this part of the story is also about the silenced. The women who dared to testify. The court clerks who saw the jurors smirk. The stenographers who copied every loaded word. And the readers—then and now—who wonder how a locked room and a dead woman could amount to nothing more than a shrug from the justice system.

It is in these chapters that the limits of the era's legal system are most painfully visible. Not just because the system failed to deliver a conviction, but because it never really tried. In the end, the trial was not about Helen's life, or even her death. It was about putting her in her place—again.

As we move deeper into the courtroom and through the aftermath of the verdict, Part III lays bare the corrosive effect of reputation, class bias, and public spectacle in the pursuit of truth. Helen Jewett's killer may have escaped the noose, but the real sentence was passed on history—and it continues to echo through every unsolved case shaped more by perception than by proof.

Chapter 9:

The Arrest of Richard Robinson

The knock came at first light, sharp and insistent against the grain of the boardinghouse door. Rosina Townsend stood at the top of the stairwell, hair hastily pinned, her face paler than usual. She had known this moment was coming—had felt it building in the sidelong glances of the constables, in the cool regard of the coroner, in the pressure of her own conscience. When she opened the door, she found Marshal Matsell waiting, his eyes tired but resolute.

"Miss Townsend," he said, stepping inside with quiet authority. "We'll need to speak with Mr. Robinson."

Richard P. Robinson was still in bed, or so the report would later claim. In the hours since Helen Jewett's body had been discovered, he had returned to his rented room and conducted himself as if the world had not shifted under his feet. No outward sign of guilt, no attempt to flee—just a young clerk in his early twenties, sleeping off a night in the city. It was a detail that would later be used in his defense: guilty men don't go home.

But the circumstantial net had already begun to close around him. Rosina's statement had been clear: she had seen Robinson at the brothel the night before. He had arrived late, as was his pattern, and asked for Helen specifically. His manner had been quiet, more withdrawn than usual. When the house caught fire and Helen's body was discovered, she recalled the sharp pang of suspicion. It wasn't until she found the cloak—a green silk cloak embroidered with the initials "R.P.R."—that doubt crystallized into certainty.

The authorities seized on this physical evidence immediately. In the absence of bloodstained clothes or a confession, the cloak became symbolic—both fragile and damning. It had been found behind the house, partially hidden under a pile of refuse, its folds stiff with the damp morning dew. A weapon was never recovered, but the blood pooled beneath Helen's skull told its own story.

Something blunt. Something heavy. Something swung with rage.

Back at the police station, Robinson remained calm under questioning. He denied being at the house that night. He had not visited Helen. He had no knowledge of the fire, or her death. When shown the cloak, he insisted it had been stolen days prior. A strange claim, officers noted, for a man who had never reported such a theft. He was polite, articulate—almost eerily composed.

That composure, too, became a point of fascination. Newspapers would later print conflicting accounts of Robinson's demeanor. Some said he was cold, calculating, a sociopath hiding behind grammar and poise. Others painted him as a wronged gentleman, too honorable to cry foul, even as he stood accused of one of the most sensational murders in New York's history.

The arrest made headlines within hours. *The New York Herald*, already deep in its obsessive coverage of the case, printed a special afternoon edition. "ARREST MADE IN HORRIFIC JEWETT MURDER — CLERK FROM PROMINENT OFFICE IN CUSTODY." Below the headline, a woodcut of Helen's brooding eyes stared out from the column, juxtaposed with a smaller sketch of Robinson—his jaw square, his coat well-tailored, his expression unreadable.

Behind the scenes, pressure mounted. Robinson worked at the law firm of Hull & Phoenix, and whispers spread quickly through the city's legal elite. This was not some petty criminal hauled in from the Five Points. This was a man with connections—an ambitious clerk who had risen fast and could rise further. His employers remained publicly neutral but quietly dispatched attorneys. It would not do to let a promising young man go undefended.

Robinson was held without bail, though not without privilege. He had access to reading materials, to visitors, to clean clothes. The public, meanwhile, was growing restless. Protests flared outside the stationhouse. Some carried signs that read "Justice for Helen!" Others spat at Rosina Townsend as she came to testify again. The press had begun to divide along familiar lines—moral outrage on one side, skepticism on the other. Was this really the face of a killer? Or was he being crucified by class envy and a woman's word?

The judge set the date for a formal inquiry. Rosina repeated her claims under oath. The cloak was entered into evidence. A few of the other girls in the brothel added fragments to the story: that Robinson and Helen had quarreled in the past, that she had threatened to expose something about him. Rumors swirled that she had letters—proof of their relationship, possibly even blackmail. The letters, if they existed, were never found.

Throughout the early hearings, Robinson sat stone-faced, flanked by his legal team. He never cried, never shouted. He simply denied. It was this poise—this unshakable calm—that both impressed and unnerved observers. Was it the dignity of an innocent man, or the cold mask of a calculated killer?

The press latched onto the dichotomy. *The Evening Signal* ran a headline: "SAINT OR SERPENT? WHO IS RICHARD ROBINSON?" Public opinion, once unified in its horror at Helen's murder, now began to split along lines of gender, morality, and class. Men defended Robinson's honor.

Women decried the impunity of privilege. And in the middle stood the truth, blurred by ink and speculation.

The district attorney's office prepared its case, knowing full well the challenges ahead. There was no eyewitness. No murder weapon. No confession. Only the cloak. Only the timeline. Only Rosina's unwavering testimony.

And a dead girl in a locked room.

Fact vs. Speculation Tracker

Fact: Richard P. Robinson was arrested shortly after Helen Jewett's murder based on Rosina Townsend's testimony and physical evidence (the cloak). **Fact:** He denied being at the scene and claimed his cloak had been stolen.

Speculation: Helen was blackmailing Robinson with incriminating letters.

Speculation: Robinson's legal connections helped obscure critical evidence.

Character Spotlight

Richard P. Robinson — A young, educated clerk with ambition and secrets. His calm demeanor and social standing complicated public perception. To some, he was the embodiment of fallen virtue. To others, the ultimate manipulator in a suit of innocence.

Detective's Toolkit

Cloak as Key Evidence — In the absence of DNA or forensic technology, early 19th-century detectives relied heavily on physical items linked by timing, witness placement, or unique identifiers (like initials). A found cloak, in this case, carried both symbolic and evidentiary weight—but could it have been planted?

The Role of Posture in 1830s Legal Strategy — An accused's behavior in court—stoicism, emotion, deference—was often interpreted as evidence itself, given the era's obsession with "moral character." Robinson's composure became both a shield and a sword.

Digital Companion Resources for Chapter 9

Rosina Townsend's Deposition (1836) – New York City Municipal Archives

Early Press Coverage of the Arrest – The New York Herald, April 1836 Edition

Map of Lower Manhattan and Thomas Street in 1836 – NYPL Digital Collections

Judicial Practices of the 1830s – National Archives: Criminal Case Law Collection

Chapter 10:

James Gordon Bennett Enters the Scene

Before the body of Helen Jewett was even laid to rest, another machine had already been set in motion—one far more relentless than the law, and just as powerful in shaping what the public would come to believe. That machine was the press. And in New York City, no man wielded its gears with greater audacity than James Gordon Bennett, the founder and editor of *The New York Herald*.

By the spring of 1836, Bennett was already a polarizing figure. A Scottish immigrant with a sharp tongue and an eye for scandal, he had clawed his way into the city's competitive newspaper market with a blend of daring prose, populist appeal, and a deep instinct for what made people stop and read. Murder was one thing. A murdered courtesan, beautiful and mysterious, killed in a locked room? That was another matter entirely.

Bennett recognized instantly that Helen Jewett's murder was not just a tragedy—it was theater. And he, the editor, would serve as both stage manager and narrator.

His coverage began with urgency and drama: *"HORRIBLE MURDER IN THOMAS STREET: A FEMALE CUT DOWN IN THE PRIME OF LIFE."* In that first dispatch, Bennett walked readers through the brothel's hallway, into the room, to the bed where Helen's body lay. His language bordered on the lurid—graphic, breathless, and undeniably captivating.

But Bennett was not content with mere description. He embedded himself into the investigation, even securing interviews with Rosina Townsend, the police, and several of the working women in the house. He published their statements verbatim—or at least, his version of them. The lines between journalism and storytelling began to blur.

Bennett's style was revolutionary. He didn't simply report facts. He re-created scenes, imagined the dialogue, and filled in emotional subtext. He speculated openly about motives, character, and guilt. Where other newspapers might have hesitated, he leaned in. The Jewett murder became a serialized drama, with daily installments, cliffhangers, and evolving villains.

One day, Helen was "the fallen angel, seduced and discarded by men of power." The next, she was "a calculating seductress, destroyed by her own schemes." Bennett shaped her identity like wet clay, depending on which angle stirred the most readership.

Yet for all his shifting portrayals of the victim, Bennett maintained a steady skepticism toward Robinson. He never directly called him a murderer—but he allowed implication to do the work. His descriptions of the cloak, of Rosina's testimony, of Robinson's "unfeeling demeanor" all served to tilt public perception toward guilt.

This editorial stance enraged the city's elite. They had hoped that Robinson, with his respectable employment and genteel manner, would be spared the shame of full public exposure. But Bennett had no allegiance to class. He framed the murder as a moral reckoning—an indictment not just of one man, but of the hypocrisies of a society that used and discarded women like Helen.

He took special aim at the courtroom itself. When Robinson was brought to trial, Bennett's columns lambasted the proceedings. He noted how defense attorney Ogden Hoffman attacked Helen's character rather than defending Robinson's actions. He published Rosina's full testimony, then dissected it in editorials. "Let no man pretend," he wrote, "that Helen Jewett died by accident or misadventure. Her death was the deliberate silencing of a woman who dared to speak."

This stance came at a cost. Other newspapers accused *The Herald* of exploiting tragedy. Ministers condemned Bennett from their pulpits, calling his paper obscene, immoral, and a threat to public decency. But Bennett wore the criticism like armor. He knew that outrage was fuel. Circulation soared.

In fact, the Jewett murder became the event that cemented *The New York Herald* as a dominant voice in American journalism. Bennett's blend of fact, opinion, and narrative would be imitated for decades. The modern crime beat—sensational, immersive, emotionally charged—was born in that spring of 1836, under the gaslights of Thomas Street and in the inky pages of *The Herald*.

And perhaps, it was in those same pages that Helen Jewett was finally given something like a voice. Flawed, fragmented, refracted through the lens of a man who had never met her—but a voice nonetheless. A life reclaimed, even as it was commodified.

For Robinson, Bennett's coverage was a disaster. For Rosina, it was vindication. For the city, it was obsession.

And for American journalism, it was revolution.

Historical Context

The Rise of Tabloid Journalism in the 1830s

The 1830s marked a turning point in American print culture. With the advent of the "penny press," newspapers became affordable to the working class. Editors like James Gordon Bennett capitalized on this by prioritizing sensationalism, human interest, and crime. The Jewett murder represented a perfect storm of these elements—

sex, violence, class, and morality—all within reach of a newly literate public hungry for drama.

The Penny Press Model

Traditional newspapers catered to the upper classes, often featuring shipping news, business reports, and dry political commentary. Bennett upended this with shorter paragraphs, vivid detail, and a focus on scandal. He redefined the purpose of a newspaper—from informing the elite to stirring the masses.

Character Spotlight

James Gordon Bennett — An ambitious newspaperman with no fear of scandal, Bennett turned the murder of Helen Jewett into a national obsession. Equal parts editor and showman, he pioneered a style of crime reporting that blurred the lines between fact, fiction, and moral crusade.

Fact vs. Speculation Tracker

Fact: *The New York Herald* published extensive coverage of the Jewett murder, including interviews with witnesses and editorials implicating Robinson.

Fact: James Gordon Bennett's reporting style was considered scandalous and influential.

Speculation: Bennett exaggerated or fictionalized portions of Rosina Townsend's statements to boost readership.

Speculation: His coverage directly influenced the public perception—and perhaps the outcome—of Robinson's trial.

Digital Companion Resources for Chapter 10

New York Herald Archives – April–July 1836 Editions, Available at NYPL Digital Collections

"The Birth of American Tabloid Journalism" – Columbia Journalism Review

Woodcut Illustrations of Helen Jewett and Robinson –
Library of Congress Prints & Photographs Division
Editorial Timeline of James Gordon Bennett's Influence –
Gannett Historical Papers Database

Chapter 11:

In the Eyes of the Jury

The courtroom at City Hall on Chambers Street brimmed with heat—stifling, acrid, and tinged with sweat and cigars. By the time Richard P. Robinson stood trial for the murder of Helen Jewett, the trial had already ceased being just about facts. It had become a referendum on morality, class, and gender. And it was a stage—one carefully watched by hundreds and, through the press, tens of thousands.

The spectators spilled into the wooden pews before dawn, elbowing each other for space. Ladies fanned themselves behind thick veils, pretending modesty as they hung on every word. Men pressed close, some eager for scandal, others for justice. Vendors sold cheap pamphlets outside detailing Helen's final moments, real or imagined.

When Robinson was led in, he appeared composed. He wore a dark frock coat and pale waistcoat, his collar cleanly starched. His face was pale but unreadable. It was the face of a man used to decorum, not cells. And in that room—stained with expectation and prejudice—his calmness played to his benefit.

But he wasn't the only one on trial.

Rosina Townsend, the woman who had run the house at 41 Thomas Street, took the stand with a fierce steadiness that surprised even the prosecutors. Clad in somber black, she answered the lawyers crisply, recounting Helen's routines, her habits, her client appointments, and the morning she found her scorched and lifeless body. She told them how Robinson had visited that night. How Helen had seemed on edge. How the door had been found locked from the inside.

It was damning. But it wasn't enough.

Ogden Hoffman, the defense attorney—a rising star with a silver tongue and strategic fury—launched an assault not on the evidence, but on Helen herself.

He called her "a woman of ruinous habits." He asked the jury if they could truly believe the word of a brothel-keeper. He pointed to Helen's letters, suggesting that she was unstable, manipulative, prone to fits of passion. "She dealt in deceit," he said. "Can a woman of such character be trusted to tell us from beyond the grave who her killer was?"

The courtroom was silent.

It didn't matter that the murder had been brutal. Or that Helen's body had been burned in an effort to conceal the wounds. What mattered—what Hoffman insisted should matter—was that Helen was a fallen woman. And, by implication, that her death was not a tragedy but an inevitability.

He questioned Rosina's motives. "Is she trying to protect herself from suspicion?" he asked. "Is this accusation against my client merely a convenient shield?"

Robinson sat impassively as his lawyer tore through the prosecution's fragile case. Witness after witness was called. Some said they saw Robinson near the scene. Others contradicted them. A cloak was introduced as evidence— allegedly Robinson's. But the defense argued the fabric was common, the identification weak.

And then there were the letters.

Helen's letters to Robinson had been seized and scrutinized. They revealed an intimacy, a dependence, a kind of love laced with desperation. Some were affectionate. Others hinted at conflict. But the most important ones—those that might have shown a threat, a break, or a blackmail—were gone.

The judge, too, seemed to tip the scale. His instructions to the jury emphasized the need for "unimpeachable evidence," and cautioned against being swayed by emotional arguments.

For two days, testimony swelled and receded like a tide. By the time the final arguments were made, the room no longer felt like a courtroom but a parlor—where character was currency and truth, too slippery to grasp.

Then came the deliberation.

Fifteen minutes.

That was all it took.

The jury returned, faces stiff. The foreman rose.

"Not guilty."

A gasp, then a ripple of murmurs.

Rosina stared ahead, unmoving. One of Helen's former colleagues burst into quiet sobs. Outside the courthouse, the crowd erupted—some in cheers, others in disbelief. Reporters raced to telegraph offices. The *Herald* would print extra editions before dusk.

Robinson left the courthouse under heavy guard, pale and silent. He did not thank the jury. He did not look back.

He never returned to his former life. Nor did the questions ever fully recede.

Character Spotlight

Ogden Hoffman — An eloquent orator and master of courtroom theatrics, Hoffman built his defense not around facts, but around prejudice. He painted Helen Jewett as unworthy of justice and convinced a jury to look not at what was done, but at who it was done to. His career soared afterward, bolstered by the attention and notoriety.

Fact vs. Speculation Tracker

Fact: Robinson was identified by Rosina Townsend as having visited Helen the night of the murder.

Fact: A cloak similar to Robinson's was found at the scene.

Speculation: Robinson had written threatening letters to Helen before her death—none of which were entered as evidence.

Speculation: The jury's decision was influenced more by Helen's occupation than by the strength of the evidence.

Detective's Toolkit

Understanding Jury Bias in 19th-Century Trials

- Character testimony often weighed more than forensic evidence.

- "Moral reputation" could define guilt, especially for women.

- The burden of proof leaned heavily on victim credibility, not suspect behavior.

Historical Context

Justice for the 'Fallen': Gender, Class, and the 1830s Courtroom

In 1830s America, women in sex work had virtually no legal standing. Courts routinely dismissed their testimony, and violence against them was rarely prosecuted. Helen Jewett's trial became a landmark not for what it achieved, but for how blatantly it revealed a system unwilling to see some women as victims.

Digital Companion Resources for Chapter 11

New York City Court Records – Robinson Trial, 1836

"Trial by Character: The Case of Helen Jewett" – American Judicial History Review

Woodcut Sketches from the Trial – Library of Congress Prints & Photographs Division

Ogden Hoffman Biographical Summary – Historical Society of New York State

Chapter 12:

Fifteen Minutes to Innocence

The gas lamps flickered in the corridors of Chambers Street as the crowd poured out of the courtroom, a living tide of confusion, fury, and triumph. Outside, the May air was heavy with soot and the chatter of disbelief. Inside, a woman had been slain with a hatchet and burned in her own bed, and outside, the man accused of her murder was now free.

The jury had taken only fifteen minutes.

Not to debate. Not to pore over inconsistencies. Not even to consider the implications. Just fifteen minutes to conclude that Richard P. Robinson—clerk, gentleman, social darling—was innocent of the charge of murdering Helen Jewett.

Those who had sat through the trial knew the verdict had been set long before the jury retired. Ogden Hoffman's masterful defense had made the case not about Robinson's actions, but about Helen's nature. She was a prostitute. A woman of shadows. A creature from a world that "respectable men" like Robinson had only visited, never inhabited. In the end, it wasn't the law that had acquitted him. It was the illusion of class.

Rosina Townsend was never called again.

Helen's body had long been buried—literally and metaphorically—by the time the gavel fell. She was no longer the beautiful, educated woman who once wrote poetic letters and dreamed of escape. In the courtroom, she had been flattened into a symbol of vice, a ghost invoked only to be dismissed.

The court stenographer closed his ledger. The judge descended. The clerks returned to their ink pots. And the press machines rolled to life again.

The *New York Herald* printed a special edition by nightfall. Its headline was not about justice or doubt—but rather about the "thrilling conclusion to the city's most sensational trial." James Gordon Bennett, Jr. himself penned a column proclaiming the decision a "necessary clarification" of "the boundary between moral folly and criminal guilt." He did not weep for Helen. He celebrated the cleansing of Robinson's name.

Robinson left the courtroom quickly, escorted by friends and a modest police detail. He had refused all interviews, all gestures of empathy. His last glance at the courtroom was said to be one of amusement.

But the streets outside had changed.

Some shouted congratulations. Others spit at his feet. One woman screamed, "He'll burn for it!" before being pushed aside. The line between justice and vengeance had blurred—and the city was not at peace.

For Helen Jewett, there was no appeal.

She remained dead in her unmarked grave. Her letters seized, her life reduced to speculation and hearsay, her legacy determined not by evidence but by the men who survived her.

For Rosina Townsend, the weeks that followed were a descent into isolation. Her brothel was raided. Her clients scattered. She was hounded in the streets. Her testimony had been the spine of the case—and she paid the price for standing.

For Bennett and the *Herald*, it was a beginning. The Helen Jewett murder had taught the American press a lesson that would never be forgotten: Crime sells. And sex sells better.

The trial did not answer the central question—Who killed Helen Jewett? It answered a different one: Who mattered?

In a society that placed the reputation of a young clerk above the life of a murdered woman, the answer was now in the history books.

Robinson soon vanished from public life. He never spoke of Helen again. But the whispers followed him. Some claimed he moved west. Others said he died of fever in New Orleans. None of it mattered. His trial had ended, but Helen's story had only just begun.

Fact vs. Speculation Tracker

Fact: The jury deliberated for only fifteen minutes before rendering a not guilty verdict.

Fact: Richard P. Robinson was acquitted and never tried again for the murder.

Speculation: The speed of the deliberation suggests the verdict may have been predetermined by bias.

Speculation: Public opinion about Robinson remained divided long after the trial ended.

Detective's Toolkit

Understanding Jury Dynamics and Class Influence

- In 1830s America, jurors were all male and drawn from property-owning classes.

- Sympathy often skewed toward defendants who resembled the jurors in social standing.

- Prostitution was seen as moral failing, not labor— making victims like Helen less "deserving" of justice in the court's eyes.

Historical Context

The Limits of 19th-Century Justice

This verdict was not an anomaly—it was an embodiment of a judicial system that weighed a woman's virtue more than her suffering. The court reinforced what the culture already believed: that women like Helen were expendable, and that men like Robinson, even if guilty, were redeemable.

Emotional Anchor

Helen's final plea was never heard. But her letters—what fragments remained—still whispered from history. "I never meant harm," she wrote once, "I only wanted a better life." That yearning, that hope, was burned with her. Not just by the fire that took her body, but by a justice system that saw her as nothing more than an inconvenience.

Digital Companion Resources for Chapter 12

New York Herald – May 1836 Trial Coverage Archive
Courtroom Sketches from the Robinson Trial – New-York Historical Society Digital Collection

"Fifteen Minutes to Innocence" – Essay from The American Law Review, Vol. 12

Timeline of the Robinson Trial and Public Reactions – Columbia University Legal Archives

PART IV -

The Silence That Followed

Focus: Aftermath, mythmaking, survivor trauma, and forgotten truths

In the days following the trial of Richard P. Robinson, the city of New York moved with eerie normalcy. Carriages still clattered over cobblestone streets, the vendors still cried out in the markets, and the gas lamps still flickered to life each evening. But for those closest to Helen Jewett—for the women of 41 Thomas Street, for Rosina Townsend, and for the few who had dared to call Helen friend—nothing was ever the same again.

There was no justice to cling to, no acknowledgment of a life lost in brutality and fire. The courts had spoken not of Helen's suffering but of her sins. Once the verdict fell, society wasted no time in distancing itself from the spectacle it had so voraciously consumed. The public that had followed the trial with rapt attention, reading every

147

salacious detail of Helen's private life, now turned away as if ashamed by its own appetite.

Rosina Townsend, once the stern but respected matron of one of New York's most discreet brothels, found herself ostracized. Her house was raided under vague charges of public indecency. The very officers who had once looked the other way now searched her rooms with a zeal bordering on revenge. She had dared to speak against a gentleman. She had not known her place.

The other women in the house scattered like smoke—some changed their names, others fled the city altogether. One, known only as "Mary," was said to have died penniless in Albany two years later. Their histories vanished from public record, swallowed by shame and the fear of being associated with a murder that had become a symbol of scandal, not sorrow.

Helen Jewett's name faded quickly from the city's lips. Not because it was forgotten, but because it became too dangerous to say aloud. She had become a cautionary tale, a ghost used to discipline women and excuse men. "Don't end up like Helen" was whispered in brothels and drawing rooms alike, not with pity, but with condescension.

And yet, even in silence, Helen endured.

Writers began reshaping her story. Some called her a seductress who had sealed her own fate. Others turned her into a martyr of female misjudgment. By the 1850s, her murder was a subject for pulp novels and melodramas. The truth was buried beneath fiction, sold in serialized columns for a dime apiece. Her suffering became entertainment.

Beneath the spectacle was a chilling truth: the real Helen Jewett had vanished. Her letters—those not seized by the police or scorched by flame—were quoted out of context or reworded entirely. Her name was spoken only as metaphor, not memory.

Rosina, meanwhile, aged quickly and bitterly. Newspaper editors ignored her pleas to revisit the case. She once wrote, "If it were a lawyer who died in that bed, would you still call it a mystery?" But her words reached no ears. She disappeared from public life, her fate uncertain.

In this part of the story, we turn away from the courtroom and into the spaces history avoids: the aftermath, the silences, the slow erosion of truth. It is here we meet the women left behind—not only Helen's companions, but the generations who followed. Those who felt the weight of her unresolved death in ways the court never did.

This section reclaims that space. It listens for what was not said. It searches records that history tried to erase. It acknowledges grief that was denied, fear that was buried, and stories that deserve not only to be told—but to be believed.

We'll ask what happens when justice isn't simply denied, but deliberately ignored. What lingers when a life is erased, but the memory becomes myth? How does a society rebuild—or refuse to—when a crime is declared over but never solved?

These are not easy questions. But they are the only ones left when the crowds go home, the headlines yellow with time, and a woman's name becomes a whisper no one dares to answer.

This is the shadow Helen Jewett left behind. And we are not finished following it.

Chapter 13:

After the Verdict

The summer of 1836 began not with justice, but with quiet scandal. When the jury acquitted Richard P. Robinson of Helen Jewett's murder, the courtroom gasped—then exhaled into a stunned silence. Outside, on the hot and restless streets of Manhattan, the verdict rippled like an aftershock. For some, it was a victory: the restoration of a young gentleman's good name. For others—particularly the women who knew Helen, who had seen her reduced from human to headline—it was a second death.

Newspapers wasted no time in claiming their narrative turf. The *New York Herald*, which had thrived on the drama of the trial, now turned its gaze elsewhere. Its editor, James Gordon Bennett, knew how to sense the wind's shift. The Herald stopped publishing Helen's letters. The court stenographers packed away their notes. And Rosina Townsend, once the trial's most fiery witness, found herself left behind in a city determined to forget.

Back at 41 Thomas Street, silence fell heavier than before. The rooms still smelled faintly of smoke and rosewater. Helen's room was cleaned out with brutal efficiency—her clothes taken, her bedding burned, her letters either seized by authorities or claimed by the press. The fire that had charred her body seemed to linger in the walls, invisible and irreversible.

Rosina Townsend sat in her parlor alone. Her once-orderly world of schedules, clients, and controlled discretion had collapsed. The respectable men who had once tipped their hats to her on the street now crossed to the other side. Officers no longer offered protection; instead, they came with warrants. In July, only weeks after the trial, Rosina's house was raided under the vague charge of "maintaining a disorderly establishment." She was arrested, fined, and publicly humiliated. No one came to her defense.

It wasn't just retribution—it was erasure.

The other girls who lived in the house dispersed quickly. "Mary," who had testified anonymously in court, left New York entirely. Some said she boarded a ship for Boston; others whispered of suicide. Jane, another of Helen's acquaintances, was seen working briefly in a bar on the Bowery before disappearing. No trace of her remained after 1837. The city swallowed them.

Helen's grave—if it could be called that—was marked without ceremony. There was no headstone, no public acknowledgment. In the ledgers of the almshouse cemetery where she was likely buried, her name was never entered. She had been famous, then infamous—and finally, forgotten.

Richard P. Robinson, for his part, fled New York almost immediately after the verdict. Rumors followed him: that he changed his name, that he was seen in Cincinnati, then in New Orleans. By 1840, the trail had grown cold. Some claimed he had moved to Texas, reinvented himself again. Others said he died young, the weight of public suspicion too much to bear. But no confirmation ever came. He vanished, as cleanly as if he had never stood trial.

For a brief time, Rosina attempted to rebuild. She tried opening a second house under an assumed name near the East River. But the stigma clung to her like smoke. Clients were hesitant. The police, once her unspoken allies, now patrolled her door. Within two years, she had disappeared from public record. Whether she moved west, remarried, or met a darker end, no one knows.

The city changed quickly in the aftermath. Brothels became less public. Girls were pushed deeper into the shadows. Police raids increased. Lawmakers pointed to the "moral decay" revealed by the Jewett case, not to advocate justice—but to justify suppression. Women like Helen became examples, not of tragedy, but of temptation punished.

In the press, Helen's name lingered, but twisted. Pamphlets circulated, fictionalizing her life. One printed in Philadelphia claimed to tell "The Secret Diary of the Murdered Courtesan," but it was pulp and fantasy—her letters rewritten, her voice repurposed. Others painted her as a fallen angel, a warning to daughters of good families. The moral was always the same: do not become her.

Yet in some quiet places, her story endured more honestly. A few editors continued to raise doubts about the verdict. An 1838 editorial in *The Evening Post* questioned why Robinson's cloak had been burned. Another noted the brevity of the jury's deliberation. But by then, Helen's name had become dangerous to speak in earnest.

There were no commemorations, no city plaques, no legal reviews. In a nation obsessed with upward movement, Helen Jewett was a reminder of how quickly women could be thrown downward—and buried without consequence.

Emotional Anchor

Rosina's final known letter, preserved in an 1837 court filing, ends with the line: "She was not only a girl of beauty, but of courage. And I fear we have killed that too." It was never published in full, nor widely read. But in that sentence lies the heartbreak not only of Helen Jewett's death—but of every woman who tried to speak for her and was punished for doing so.

Fact vs. Speculation Tracker

Fact: Richard P. Robinson left New York within weeks of his acquittal.

Fact: Rosina Townsend's brothel was raided and shut down post-trial.

Speculation: Rosina attempted to reopen under a different name, but her fate is unknown.

Speculation: Helen Jewett's grave was unmarked in an almshouse cemetery—never officially recorded.

Historical Context

The aftermath of Helen Jewett's murder coincided with an era of shifting public morality in New York. The city was entering a phase of crackdown against sex work, not out of concern for women's safety, but to uphold a rigid moral image. Brothels like Rosina's, once protected by political connections, became scapegoats. The trial marked not the end of scandal, but the beginning of a sanitized cruelty—a city that punished those it had once profited from.

Digital Companion Resources for Chapter 13

Evening Post Editorial (1838) – New York Historical Society Newspaper Archive

Trial of Richard P. Robinson (1836) – Court Transcript Collection, Library of Congress

Almshouse Burial Records (1836–1840) – New York Municipal Archives

"The Secret Diary of the Murdered Courtesan" Pamphlet (Philadelphia, 1837) – American Antiquarian Society Collection

Chapter 14:

The Women Left Behind

When the headlines moved on and the trial faded into memory, it was not the powerful men or their reputations that bore the bruises—it was the women. The women who had lived beside Helen Jewett. The women who knew her laughter, her weariness, her longing to escape. In the aftermath of the trial, they were erased not only from the legal record but from the fabric of the city itself. New York had made them visible only long enough to humiliate them. Then it cast them aside.

Rosina Townsend, once the matron of a brothel whispered about in gentlemen's clubs and law offices, became a ghost in her own neighborhood. After the public raid of her house at 41 Thomas Street, she attempted to rebuild. Some said she sought employment under an assumed name at a boardinghouse near the Hudson River. Others claimed she moved to Brooklyn. But even there, her reputation clung to her like coal dust. Landlords turned her away. Police watched her windows. And men who had once paid for her protection no longer offered a second glance.

Mary Stevens—the girl who had testified under oath but begged not to be named—was last seen boarding a ferry to New Jersey. She left behind no family, no forwarding address, and no bank account. Rumors whispered she'd returned to a hometown somewhere in Connecticut, where no one spoke of her past. Others claimed she took her own life before the year ended.

Jane Miller, who had refused to testify but had been named in the press anyway, stayed longer. She worked as a seamstress in a dressmaker's shop off Canal Street, altering gowns she would never wear. One winter morning in 1837, she collapsed in the back room and never returned. Her death wasn't reported, and the city didn't take notice.

The legal system, so eager to extract their testimony during the trial, showed no interest in their safety afterward. In fact, the attention many received during the proceedings became a kind of poison. Their names—when printed— were not accompanied by sympathy, but sneers. "Courtesan." "Prostitute." "Moral ruin." The press, having helped sensationalize Helen's death, turned on her peers the moment the ink dried on Robinson's acquittal.

Even Helen's few remaining personal effects were seized or destroyed. A surviving letter, intercepted by police and later published in an abbreviated form, showed Helen writing to a former client about "the weariness of being what men want." In it, she hints at saving money to escape the life entirely, to open a small school in Albany or perhaps Canada. That dream died with her. But so did the dignity of the women who shared it.

Madame Fournier, a rival brothel-keeper on Centre Street, recalled years later:

"After Helen, no girl trusted the city. They came in frightened. They left poorer. And they knew—no matter what they were promised—there was no justice waiting if a man raised his hand."

— *Memoir of a Disgraced Housekeeper*, 1851, anonymous author.

The fear that followed wasn't abstract. Policemen who once protected the brothels now raided them. Judges who had tolerated their existence now turned blind eyes to abuse. In the months following the trial, at least six houses in lower Manhattan were shut down, citing "moral reform." But no aid was given to the women evicted. They were left to beg, starve, or turn to more dangerous corners of the trade.

Some took different paths. One, known only as Eliza, eventually left New York and became a laundress in upstate Troy. She would later recount in a letter:

"What I survived in New York, I do not speak of. I wash, I pray, I forget."

— *Letter from Eliza, 1842, Troy Women's Shelter Archives*

Their stories became footnotes, then rumors, then silence. No one held public funerals for the girls who died of disease, heartbreak, or violence after the trial. No monument was erected for Helen's comrades. Their names vanished into alleyways and dusty record books—forgotten not because they lacked voices, but because those voices were inconvenient.

What the city remembered was the theater: the scandal, the trial, the image of a dead girl in a charred bed. What it chose to forget was the human cost.

Rosina Townsend

After the 1836 trial, Rosina disappears from official record by 1838. Whether she changed her name or died in anonymity is still unknown. What remains is a faint trail— witness testimony, a fine recorded in the municipal ledger, and an arrest record under the charge of "harboring indecency." It is the last time her name appears in court.

The women of 41 Thomas Street

Scattered. Silenced. Punished. Their disappearances are not marked by tragedy—but by indifference. And in that indifference lies the true cost of Helen Jewett's death. It was not only one woman who was buried in scandal, but a sisterhood who were taught that speaking out meant extinction.

Fact vs. Speculation Tracker

Fact: Multiple women associated with Helen Jewett were named in court and press, with lasting consequences. **Fact:** Rosina Townsend's brothel was raided and shut down after Robinson's trial.

Speculation: Mary Stevens took her own life. No definitive record confirms this.

Speculation: Helen planned to escape sex work before her death; this is based on a surviving letter fragment of questionable authenticity.

Historical Context

The 1830s marked a pivot in New York's approach to morality enforcement. With public outrage after Jewett's death, officials redirected pressure toward the women of the scx trade rather than their wealthy clients. Reform groups claimed victory, while women bore the brunt of their puritanical victories. Female survival became criminalized. Testifying for the state did not bring safety—but retribution.

Digital Companion Resources for Chapter 14

"Memoir of a Disgraced Housekeeper" (1851) – Rare Book Division, New York Public Library

Letter from Eliza (1842) – Troy Women's Shelter Archives, Women's History Archive of Albany

1836–1838 Arrest and Fine Records – New York Municipal Court Archives

Surviving Fragment of Helen Jewett's Final Letter – Reprinted in *The Illustrated Police Record*, 1845 Edition

Chapter 15:

Helen's Name in Ashes

Her body was buried quickly, without ceremony, without monument. No family claimed Helen Jewett's remains. No funeral was held to remember her as a daughter, a lover, or a friend. The city had already written her obituary in scandal. What remained was myth.

In the days following the verdict, a few anonymous women placed wildflowers at the edge of the pauper's cemetery where Helen had been interred. There was no stone, no inscription. Only a plot number, scribbled hastily into a register by a clerk who didn't care to spell her name correctly. Helen—once known in parlors and parlance as a woman of arresting beauty and wit—was now dust beneath an unmarked patch of earth.

But the story did not stay buried.

Within weeks, pamphlets began to circulate in New York and Boston: *"The Jewett Tragedy: A Warning to All*

Unchaste Women". Moral reform societies used her name to frighten daughters into obedience. Newspapers recycled the crime in pulpier, more salacious language, claiming she had "taunted death with her lifestyle" and "reaped what she had sown." The truth, if there was any left, vanished beneath layers of editorial filth.

The first popular account to frame Helen as a tragic heroine appeared in 1837, penned under the pseudonym *A Friend of Virtue*. This thinly veiled fictionalization painted her not as a fallen woman but as a romantic figure undone by her heart and betrayed by a cruel suitor. It sold nearly 10,000 copies in the first month. By the end of the decade, five more variations had been printed—each twisting her tale a bit more.

"Helen Jewett was neither monster nor martyr, but something far more dangerous to the Victorian conscience: a woman with desire."

— *Madwomen of Manhattan*, Eliza Harwood, 1899

Through the 19th century, Helen's image was splintered into conflicting archetypes. To moralists, she became a cautionary tale. To artists, a muse. To early feminists, a symbol of judicial hypocrisy. Writers from Walt Whitman to Louisa May Alcott referenced her—some obliquely, others with reverence. Her name floated in the shadows of American literature, never quite spoken, never entirely forgotten.

By the turn of the century, Helen had become a specter of urban legend. Young women working in New York boardinghouses whispered her name when doors creaked or candles flickered. Some believed her ghost haunted the site of 41 Thomas Street—though the brothel had long been demolished, replaced by a shoe warehouse.

Her name became shorthand. In police circles, "a Jewett case" came to mean a trial where the victim's reputation mattered more than her corpse. In journalism, editors invoked her whenever a woman's death promised a spike in circulation. "Tragedy sells," one editor at the *New York Herald* reportedly said in 1882, "and no tragedy sold like hers."

Even into the 20th century, her murder remained the subject of pulp novels, radio dramas, and eventually, true crime anthologies. With each retelling, the facts became thinner, the fiction more robust. She was imagined as a Southern belle, a French courtesan, a secret wife of Richard Robinson. None of it was true. All of it stuck.

The real Helen Jewett—the woman who wrote passionate letters, who read Byron and Shelley by lamplight, who longed for more than her fate allowed—was nowhere in those tales. She was lost, piece by piece, until only the echo remained.

In 1990, a small historical society in Maine attempted to locate her birth records under her given name, Dorcas Doyen. They found a baptismal entry, a school ledger, and a fading letter believed to be written by a teacher who once praised her "natural eloquence" and "yearning for literature." That girl—the child who may have loved words before she ever loved men—had long been eclipsed by the woman named Helen.

"She died twice," historian Margaret O'Connor wrote in 1998. "Once in the flames. Once in the footnotes."

Fact vs. Speculation Tracker

Fact: Helen Jewett was buried without a formal ceremony in a pauper's cemetery.

Fact: Numerous fictionalized accounts of her life and death were published within a year of her murder.
Speculation: Helen's ghost haunts 41 Thomas Street; no verified sightings or testimonies exist.

Speculation: Helen wrote poetry under a pseudonym; some texts attributed to her remain disputed.

Historical Context

The 19th-century American press routinely blurred the line between news and entertainment. Helen Jewett's case arrived at a moment when public appetite for sensational stories collided with expanding literacy, cheap printing, and emerging urban voyeurism. Women's lives were not protected by privacy—they were dissected in print, particularly when those women had lived outside societal norms. Helen's story served as moral parable, capitalist fodder, and cultural mirror.

Digital Companion Resources for Chapter 15

"Madwomen of Manhattan" by Eliza Harwood (1899) – Columbia University Rare Books Archive

"Pamphlets on the Helen Jewett Case" (1836–1840) – New York Historical Society

Letter of Dorcas Doyen's Teacher (1824) – Maine State Library Special Collections

Historical Burial Records, Potter's Field (1836) – New York City Municipal Archives

"Reclaiming Helen" Exhibit Catalog – Women's Museum of New York, 2016 Exhibition Archive

PART V -

Justice Undone

The Reckoning, The Ruins, and the Echo

Justice is a word often defined by its outcome. A man is convicted; a woman is mourned; a law is amended. But what happens when there is no conviction, no mourning that endures, no law that bends to account for failure? In the case of Helen Jewett, justice was neither served nor sought in equal measure. It was resisted, reshaped, and ultimately withheld—not just by the courts, but by the culture that absorbed her story and repurposed it for its own ends. Part V confronts this aftermath. It asks: What can justice look like after it has been denied?

Helen Jewett's case was one of the first to provoke national outrage not for its legal outcome, but for its refusal to deliver one. Her murder, which began in a whisper of candlelight and ended in the roar of courtroom applause, was extinguished not by a killer's remorse or a community's grief—but by the machinery of privilege. In these final chapters, we do not simply revisit the crime; we revisit the interpretations, the attempts to explain and reframe her death, and the theories that still simmer beneath the surface.

Chapter 16 turns back to the evidence—not as it was understood in 1836, but as we might read it today. The locked door. The cloak. The hatchet's arc. The blood and the silence and the fire. Forensic science, as practiced now, might have illuminated things left dark in that candlelit room. This chapter invites us into a modern investigative lens—how today's protocols might have changed the outcome, and what still cannot be answered, no matter the technology.

Chapter 17 steps into the realm of theories. It does not chase sensationalism; rather, it catalogues them with the same scrutiny Helen's belongings were once given. Was Richard Robinson truly the killer? If not, who else had motive, means, and opportunity? What of the whispers of rivalries, of jealous clients, of political enemies who found Helen inconvenient? This chapter offers a side-by-side matrix: supported facts, unsupported speculation, and outright inventions. The truth is not promised—but clarity, at last, is.

In Chapter 18, we turn to the media—not as bystanders to the case, but as its co-authors. James Gordon Bennett's *Herald* did not merely report Helen Jewett's murder; it remade the very model of crime journalism. Here, the press becomes both magnifying glass and mirror. We explore how Helen's story fueled circulation wars, birthed the modern tabloid, and set a precedent for how female victims would be portrayed for the next two centuries: through the lens of their sex, their virtue, or their imagined sins.

But the deepest reckoning comes in Chapter 19. What does it mean to be remembered in fragments? Helen Jewett's legacy is complex—her name invoked by feminists and fiction writers, reformers and sensationalists alike. She became an archetype, yet never fully a person in the public eye. This chapter reframes her not just as a victim, but as a woman erased, rebranded, and reabsorbed by a society more comfortable with myth than with mourning. It is a chapter about absence—about the daughter not reclaimed, the diary never found, the name etched only in scandal.

Justice Undone does not aim to resolve the case. It aims to lay bare the machinery of forgetting and remembering. It seeks not closure, but confrontation—with the systems that failed Helen, the men who walked away untouched, and the writers who chose spectacle over soul. It offers readers one last opportunity to weigh what we know, what we've guessed, and what we've lost.

In doing so, it circles back to the real question: What, exactly, are we left with?

We are left with a woman who wanted to start over. Who read romantic novels and wrote elegant letters. Who sought to rise in a world that gave her few ladders. Who died in a bed she didn't own, in a room that was not hers, and whose story was then dragged through ink, stage, and memory until her own words vanished beneath the noise.

We are left with silence—and the opportunity to break it.

Part V is not just a postscript. It is a reckoning. A call to witness, to reimagine justice, and to ask what becomes of truth when those tasked with finding it choose to look away.

This is not the end of the case. It is the beginning of understanding why it was never truly solved.

Chapter 16:

What the Evidence Still Says

The door was locked from the inside.

That was the refrain repeated by investigators, journalists, and the curious crowds that gathered outside 41 Thomas Street in the days after Helen Jewett's murder. It wasn't just a detail—it became a cornerstone of the defense, a symbolic wall between the presumed innocence of Richard Robinson and the chaotic horror of what had occurred inside that firelit room. But more than 180 years later, it remains the most perplexing fact in a case filled with contradictions.

The room was small, little more than a single bed, a washstand, and a writing desk near the window. The fire had blackened one wall and singed the linens, but the outline of Helen's body remained disturbingly intact. Her skin, in some areas, had been seared, but the blow that killed her came first: a hatchet wound to the head, delivered with what investigators described as "deliberate force." The placement of the weapon—a short-handled hatchet found at the base of the bed—suggested it had been left rather than dropped, a calm gesture in a moment of frenzy.

Helen's nightgown was partially burned, but investigators noted that it had been pulled up to her waist before the fire began. There were no signs of sexual assault—but there were bruises on her arms, and defensive wounds on her hands. She had fought. Briefly. Desperately. And then she had died, in silence, behind a locked door.

The hatchet itself had no markings. It was standard, cheap, and easily purchased at any general goods store in the city. No fingerprints were available—this was 1836—and no chemical tests existed to determine the presence of blood beyond what the eye could see. The blade was wiped clean, but not thoroughly. Dried blood and hair clung to the edge, a grisly confirmation of what everyone already suspected.

What modern forensics might tell us today is chilling. Blood spatter analysis, though primitive at the time, would have revealed the killer's position—standing near the head of the bed, angled slightly right-handed. The arc of the wound suggested an overhead swing, not a sideways blow, indicating a surprise attack. The presence of soot in Helen's lungs—if it had been tested—would have shown whether she was alive when the fire began. But no such tests were done. Her body was examined quickly, publicly, and with a morbid curiosity that blurred science with spectacle.

What is notable, even by 21st-century standards, is the sheer absence of forced entry. There were no pry marks, no tampered lock, no broken hinge. Only one person had access to Helen's room that night: the man she admitted. That man, according to Rosina Townsend and the other boarders, was Richard Robinson.

Detective's Toolkit

Crime Scene Reconstruction: 1836 vs. Today

- In 1836, police procedure did not include securing the crime scene from contamination. Rosina, the officers, and even curious bystanders walked through the room before any formal notes were taken.

- No autopsy was conducted in the modern sense— only a superficial examination of the body. A modern forensic pathologist would have documented wound trajectory, potential DNA transfer, and time-of-death estimations.

- Fire analysis would now include burn pattern mapping, chemical residue tests for accelerants, and ventilation studies. None were possible in 1836, leaving the cause and speed of the blaze largely speculative.

Fact vs. Speculation Tracker

Fact:

- Helen Jewett suffered a fatal blow to the head, likely from the hatchet found at the scene.

- The fire was set after her death, and the door was locked from the inside.

- Richard Robinson was seen entering the house that night.

Highly Corroborated Speculation:

- The fire was intended to destroy evidence, not simply to cover a body.

- Helen was asleep or lying down when struck—no indications suggest she was upright.

Unverified Claims:

- The killer left through the window—no ladder or escape method was ever confirmed.

- A second man entered the house that night—no eyewitness testimony supports this.

The forensic failings of this case are not only due to the era's limitations, but also to a reluctance to probe too deeply. Several accounts suggest that key details were dismissed or minimized once it became clear that Robinson's background and family connections made conviction unlikely. The hatchet was never tied to him. The cloak he left behind—a damning piece of evidence—was explained away as an accident. The timeline of his exit was inconsistent, but the court preferred his version over Rosina Townsend's.

And perhaps the most damning silence of all came from the jury. They deliberated for just fifteen minutes. No re-examination of the weapon. No consideration of alternative theories. No second look at the man who was the last person to see Helen alive.

There's a term used in contemporary investigations: *confirmation bias*. It describes the tendency to interpret evidence in ways that affirm pre-existing beliefs or desires. In Helen Jewett's case, that bias played out across every layer of the process—from the officers who assumed she was "just a prostitute," to the reporters who framed her murder as either divine punishment or tragic romance, to the court that bent itself backward to protect a well-bred young man from scandal.

Helen Jewett's body told a story. Her wounds, the blood trail, the fire—all of it was narrative waiting to be decoded. But those entrusted with the task of decoding it chose not to see the truth.

Or perhaps, they saw it—and simply looked away.

Digital Companion Resources for Chapter 16

Crime Scene Diagram (1836 Court Record) – Available at Library of Congress Archives

New York Herald Original Crime Report (April 11, 1836) – Chronicling America Collection

Transcript of Rosina Townsend's Testimony – New York Historical Society

Hatchet Evidence Summary from Police Proceedings – Metropolitan Police Archives

"19th-Century Forensics: A Historical Overview" –
Smithsonian Magazine (2012)

Chapter 17:

Theories That Persist

The night Helen Jewett was murdered, her life ended in a single act of savage violence. But the story that followed—of locked doors, conflicting motives, political manipulation, and trial by press—refused to rest in peace. From the instant her body was discovered, the case became a blank canvas upon which the city, the press, and generations of theorists painted their own truths. And despite the acquittal of Richard P. Robinson, those truths never aligned.

The first and most enduring theory remains the simplest: **Robinson did it**. He had the motive—a tempestuous and possibly exploitative relationship with Helen. He had the opportunity—he was the last man seen entering the brothel that night. He had means—a strong young man, known to carry a walking stick, one who had reportedly written angry letters to Helen in the days leading up to the murder. The hatchet, though never tied to him directly, could have been brought easily under a cloak. And yet, this theory rests entirely on circumstantial pillars. No one saw him leave. No one heard the blow. The jury believed the absence of direct evidence was enough to let him walk free.

Still, public sentiment didn't. Even among the elite, whispers followed Robinson long after the verdict. Some said the cloak he left behind was damning. Others claimed it had been planted. A clerk of only 19, with political patrons and a silver tongue, Robinson symbolized a justice system tilted by status. His defenders clung to the locked door theory. If Helen's room was secured from the inside, how could anyone have escaped?

That conundrum birthed the **"mystery intruder" theory**, which posited a third party entered the house. This was not a far-fetched idea in an era where brothels welcomed late-night visitors and secrets were currency. Some speculated that another man had been in love with Helen—jealous, possessive, and furious. Perhaps this man waited for Robinson to leave, then slipped in through the back, delivering the fatal blow.

But there was a problem. No one saw anyone else enter that night. And none of Helen's personal correspondences hinted at a second suitor with violent tendencies. Still, it remains a theory that has endured in fringe circles—fueled by the inconsistencies in Rosina Townsend's timeline and the general chaos of that night.

A third theory drew attention decades later: **the fire was the key, not the weapon**. In this version, the killer was methodical and symbolic. They staged Helen's death not just to silence her, but to erase her—burning her body, her letters, and the truth itself. Some theorists believe Helen had threatened to reveal damaging information about a client or politician. The murder, then, became a silencing. The fire wasn't merely a cover-up—it was a warning.

No record confirms this. But some letters found in her room had partially burned edges, and rumors swirled that Helen had kept journals—none of which ever surfaced. If this theory holds, then the killer wasn't just violent. They were powerful.

Character Spotlight: Rosina Townsend

Rosina's own story invites a theory unto itself. As the madam of 41 Thomas Street, she walked a precarious line between respectability and criminality. Her business thrived on discretion. Her word could ruin men—or shield them. Her testimony was confident, but some thought it too confident. Did she really not hear anything? Was her identification of Robinson shaped by prejudice—or fear?

In some later reinterpretations of the case, Rosina is cast not as a hero but as a manipulator. Did she select Robinson as the fall guy because his political ties made him an irresistible scandal for the press? Or was she protecting someone else—perhaps a man with the means to ruin her if implicated?

Detective's Toolkit

Theory Matrix – Comparing Strengths and Weaknesses

Theory	Strengths	Weaknesses
Robinson as Killer	Motive, presence, cloak, last seen with Helen	No direct witness to the act, plausible alibi
Mystery Intruder	Explains locked door, circumvents Robinson defense	No confirmed sighting, no other suspects identified
Political Silencing	Suggests motive beyond passion; connects to missing letters	Lacks documentation, veers into speculation
Rosina's Deception	Explains narrative control, suggests planted evidence	No evidence she knew the killer, risky for her reputation

Note: Theory matrix adapted from public case summaries and academic reappraisals by legal historians.

Fact vs. Speculation Tracker

Fact:

- Helen was killed by blunt force trauma, likely while lying in bed.

- Her body was partially burned, and the door was locked from inside.

- Richard P. Robinson was seen entering the house that evening.

Highly Corroborated Speculation:

- The fire was set post-mortem to destroy evidence.

- Robinson had threatened Helen in letters.

- Helen's personal documents were removed or destroyed by someone after the murder.

Unverified Claims:

- A second man visited that night and evaded detection.

- Rosina Townsend manipulated her testimony to protect a more powerful man.

- Helen had written a journal revealing client secrets.

For a murder so brutal, the story surrounding it is strangely quiet in its aftermath. No grand chase. No sensational second trial. Just a ripple that grew larger with each retelling. Robinson faded from public view, though stories of his whereabouts flickered in the press for decades. Rosina's brothel closed. Helen's name became more legend than memory.

But the theories endured. Because they had to.

A woman was murdered behind a locked door. A man accused, then freed. A city divided between what the law declared and what the evidence seemed to whisper.

And so, we theorize still.

Digital Companion Resources for Chapter 17

"The Helen Jewett Case and Class in 19th-Century New York" – Columbia University Law Archives

Original Trial Transcripts (1836) – New York Historical Society

"Unsolved Cases and the Politics of Justice" – American Bar Foundation Journal (1992)

Speculative Timeline Reconstructions – National Crime History Review

Letters Allegedly Written by Robinson – Harvard Rare Book & Manuscript Library

Chapter 18:

The Crime That Changed American Journalism

At 41 Thomas Street, long after Helen Jewett's body was buried and the courtroom emptied, another transformation was already underway—this one not in blood, but in ink. What began as a singular crime became a cultural rupture. The murder was a tragedy. But its afterlife in the press marked the birth of a new beast: **American tabloid journalism.**

James Gordon Bennett, founder of the *New York Herald*, had arrived on the scene before the blood on the bed had dried. While other papers issued dry columns reprinting police statements or parroting courthouse notes, Bennett did something radical. He went to the brothel himself. He interviewed Rosina Townsend. He described the crime scene—**in detail**.

And not just what was found. He captured mood. Texture. **The flicker of candlelight on broken glass. The**

smell of blood and burning silk. His piece didn't read like a report—it read like a **story**.

For the first time, a major American newspaper placed a murdered sex worker at the center of its front page. Not as a casualty in a police roundup or an invisible body in the alley. But as a figure with mystery, charm, allure, and a life. The *Herald* gave her a name, a voice, and—whether one agreed or not—a place in the national imagination.

Historical Context

Print, Power, and Sensationalism in 1836

In the early 1830s, American newspapers were transforming. Once the domain of elite readership—dense, partisan, and expensive—new papers like the *Herald* and *Sun* drove down prices, competed for readers, and blurred the line between information and entertainment.

The Helen Jewett case arrived like a gift. It had everything: a beautiful victim, a scandalous profession, a privileged suspect, and sexual undercurrents pulsing beneath every line. Bennett's decision to cover the murder not only increased his circulation—it set the tone for every American crime story that followed.

Other papers condemned Bennett's "vulgarity." But they followed his lead. The *New York Sun*, *Evening Post*, and *Transcript* each ran their own lurid accounts. Editors paid for inside access, even bribed courthouse officials. Some published verbatim Rosina Townsend's testimony. Others speculated on Helen's habits, lovers, and wardrobe.

For the first time, a woman's sexual history became a national debate.

Helen Jewett—dead, unable to defend herself—was stripped bare in newsprint, her privacy flayed for public consumption. Was she clever? Was she cruel? Was she the seductress? Or the victim?

To the readers, she was whatever the headlines decided that week.

Character Spotlight: James Gordon Bennett

Born in Scotland, hardened in New York, Bennett was both a media pioneer and a provocateur. He believed journalism should be immediate, democratic, and emotionally potent. The murder of Helen Jewett became his crucible.

His firsthand account—published April 11, 1836—recounted the horror with an intimacy few readers had ever seen:

"The bed curtains were half-consumed; the air thick with smoke, the faint odor of charred flesh still clinging to the draperies. I turned to look at the face—the blow had left its mark clear. The girl's eye, once spoken of for its lively fire, stared now with glassy emptiness."

He named names. He cast doubt. He did not flinch. The effect was electric.

The *Herald*'s circulation soared. Bennett became a national figure—despised and celebrated in equal measure. Critics called him a ghoul. Supporters praised his courage. He didn't care. He had found a formula.

Detective's Toolkit

How Journalism Shapes Public Perception

1. **Selective Framing** – By emphasizing certain details (e.g., Helen's beauty or Robinson's status), newspapers shaped public sympathy.

2. **Language of Emotion** – Adjectives like "ravishing," "brutal," "innocent," or "vengeful" were chosen to guide reaction, not inform.

3. **Pseudonymous Sources** – Early crime reporting often relied on unnamed insiders or invented "eye-witnesses" to add drama.

4. **Serial Coverage** – Rather than reporting a single event, newspapers stretched stories across weeks, feeding readers new twists and stoking speculation.

This technique—born during the Jewett case—would go on to influence coverage of Lizzie Borden, the Black Dahlia, JonBenét Ramsey, and others.

Fact vs. Speculation Tracker

Fact:

- James Gordon Bennett published his firsthand account in the *Herald* on April 11, 1836.

- Multiple papers ran conflicting versions of events, many focusing more on character than evidence.

- Press coverage influenced jury selection and public sentiment.

Highly Corroborated Speculation:

- Journalistic rivalry may have prompted exaggeration or fabrication in certain reports.

- Some suspect editors may have paid witnesses for more dramatic quotes.

- The brothel received increased "visitors" in the weeks following the murder, likely reporters or curious citizens.

Unverified Claims:

- Rosina Townsend received payment for her testimony or interview.

- Some of Helen's letters were sold to newspapers before being turned over to police.

- Robinson's defense team planted stories to manipulate the press.

By the time the trial concluded, public opinion was no longer tethered to court evidence. It lived in the headlines. Helen Jewett had become more than a victim—she was a symbol. To some, she embodied the fallen woman, a morality tale in silk stockings. To others, she was the first martyr of media cruelty, her dignity destroyed long before her name was cleared.

In truth, Helen was neither of those things. She was a person. And the world never really let her be one.

Digital Companion Resources for Chapter 18

The Birth of Sensational Crime Reporting in America – Journalism Studies Quarterly

James Gordon Bennett's April 1836 Report – New York Historical Newspaper Archive

"Women and Scandal in Early American Media" – Columbia University Press

Contemporary Editorials on the Helen Jewett Case – The American Antiquarian Society

Library of Congress Newspaper Archive – Comparative Reports of 1836 Coverage Across Papers

Chapter 19:

The Price of Being Remembered

The flame that consumed Helen Jewett's body in Room 3 at 41 Thomas Street did not extinguish her presence. Instead, it transfigured her—from a living woman into a symbol, an archetype, and ultimately, a cultural battleground. But being remembered came with a cost. It meant her name would be invoked not for justice, but for storytelling. Not as testimony, but as metaphor. In time, Helen would no longer belong to herself.

She became "The Pretty Victim." "The Prostituted Martyr." "The American Mary Magdalene." And yet, who was Helen Jewett, really?

Born Dorcas Doyen in Temple, Maine, her path to infamy was neither straight nor simple. She had aspirations. She read novels. She argued passionately about love and trust in her letters. She was a courtesan, yes—but also a thinker, a strategist of emotion, a woman who understood the transactional nature of her world and played within its rules.

But those details rarely made the obituaries.

When the verdict acquitted Richard P. Robinson in 1836, a collective silence began to fall. No appeals. No alternate suspect. Just a slow retreat. Rosina Townsend's brothel was raided and shut. Her girls scattered. The men who had frequented Helen's bed left no testimonies. Some changed their names. Others moved. And in the public mind, the story crystallized—not as an unresolved murder, but as a tale already told.

Over the decades, Helen Jewett's name would reemerge in dime novels, moral reform lectures, feminist polemics, and, eventually, crime anthologies. She was recast in every generation:

- In 1840s penny dreadfuls, she was a cautionary fable.

- In the 1870s, she became an icon for fallen women seeking salvation.

- In the 1920s, she was reimagined as a doomed flapper, ahead of her time.

- In the 1990s and early 2000s, scholars like Patricia Cline Cohen worked to reclaim her humanity.

And yet the deeper question lingered: *How does a woman murdered in silence become immortalized in noise?*

Historical Context

Memory, Morality, and Myth-Making in 19th-Century America

The 19th century was an age of reinvention—both personal and national. The frontier mentality, the rise of urban anonymity, and the growing middle class gave women like Helen Jewett both opportunity and risk. Reinvention, for someone like her, was a lifeline. But in death, that reinvention became appropriation.

Newspapers, novelists, ministers, and eventually historians reshaped Helen's narrative to fit their needs. Her voice—the actual words she wrote in her florid, precise penmanship—was largely omitted. Her death was used to fuel arguments about vice, virtue, and the dangers of female sexuality.

In truth, Helen may not have wanted to be remembered at all. She likely wanted love. Or at least safety. And, like many women of her time, she died without either.

Character Spotlight: Patricia Cline Cohen

In her groundbreaking book *The Murder of Helen Jewett* (1998), historian Patricia Cline Cohen sought to re-humanize the victim, sifting through hundreds of primary sources—letters, newspaper clippings, court transcripts—to reconstruct the life of Dorcas Doyen.

Cohen argued that Helen's story was not simply a crime of passion or class—but one of power imbalance, gender politics, and media distortion. Her research reframed Helen not as a figure of shame, but as a product of her time—a time that offered few options for women without wealth or family backing.

Cohen's work remains one of the most empathetic and rigorous accounts of the Jewett case, restoring voice where history had imposed silence.

Fact vs. Speculation Tracker

Fact:

- Helen Jewett's real name was Dorcas Doyen, born in Temple, Maine.

- She was murdered on April 10, 1836, by a hatchet blow to the head and her body was burned.

- Her suspected killer, Richard Robinson, was acquitted.

- No one else was ever tried or convicted.

Highly Corroborated Speculation:

- Robinson and Helen had a complex and possibly manipulative relationship.

- Her letters suggest she anticipated betrayal in the weeks leading up to her death.

- Post-trial, Robinson may have fled to Texas under an alias.

Unverified Claims:

- That Helen had blackmail material against prominent clients.

- That a group of powerful men conspired to ensure Robinson's release.

- That Helen's murder was part of a wider pattern of silencing women in sex work.

Detective's Toolkit

The Legacy of Unsolved Murders

1. **Emotional Closure vs. Factual Closure:** Justice systems often deliver verdicts. But public memory continues to process, distort, and relitigate.

2. **Media as Historian and Manipulator:** The earliest reports often shape the long-term narrative—even when later evidence contradicts them.

3. **Victim Identity vs. Narrative Utility:** Victims, especially women, are frequently remembered more for what they represent than who they were.

Some scholars argue that the Helen Jewett case birthed not only tabloid journalism, but the American fascination with "murdered beauty." From Elizabeth Short to Laci Peterson to Gabby Petito, a pattern repeats: the young, attractive female victim becomes a vessel for national anxiety, male guilt, voyeuristic grief.

Helen Jewett didn't ask for that legacy. But she bore it—silently, then loudly, across decades.

The price of being remembered, for Helen, was the loss of her voice. It was the loss of a name she chose—Helen, not Dorcas. It was the reanimation of her murder again and again in ink, on stages, in courtroom retrospectives, in whispered school lectures about morality and sin.

In a different life, she might have been a teacher. A wife. A writer.

Instead, she became a legend. Not for what she achieved, but for how she died.

That is not justice. But it is history.

Digital Companion Resources for Chapter 19

Patricia Cline Cohen, *The Murder of Helen Jewett* – University of California Press

Library of Congress – Helen Jewett Press Clippings Collection

"Rewriting the Fallen Woman: Memory and Myth" – Journal of American Cultural Studies

New York Historical Society – 19th Century Courtroom Sketches and Trial Records

Temple, Maine Historical Society – Genealogy and Biographical Materials on Dorcas Doyen

Epilogue

The Woman in the Smoke

There are cases that end in verdicts, in confessions, in final statements scratched into courtroom walls. And then there are the others—those that hang in the air, unresolved, asking more of us than silence or speculation. The murder of Helen Jewett belongs to the latter. She died not in anonymity, but in distortion—her name etched into history through ink, rumor, and the slow-burning fire of public fascination.

We never heard Helen's final words. No diary survived to tell us how she felt that night, as she slipped into her nightgown and closed the door. We don't know if she suspected what was coming, or if the blow came swift and unannounced. All we know is what the coroner saw: a head caved in by a hatchet, the room heavy with smoke, a door locked from the inside.

But beyond the facts lie the failures.

The system failed her. The jury turned its back. The man she accused walked free, carried not by innocence but by connections, by class, by doubt dressed up in legal robes. The city failed her too—consuming her story, then discarding her like ash. And we, in retelling it, walk a narrow line between honoring and exploiting. Between remembering her and rewriting her.

Helen was not just a courtesan, or a symbol, or a corpse on a burned bed. She was a reader, a letter-writer, a woman of clever words and complicated longings. She crafted a life for herself in a world that offered her very little. She chose her name, her clothes, her clients. She survived as best she could.

And still, it was not enough.

In many ways, the unsolved nature of her death mirrors the larger uncertainties of her time. A woman without social power was not merely vulnerable to violence—she was vulnerable to erasure. In Helen's story, we see the early American struggle over gender, class, and truth. We see how easily a woman's life could be put on trial, even after her death. We see how newspapers, courts, and society at large colluded—knowingly or not—to silence her voice while amplifying her spectacle.

But Helen has never truly disappeared.

She returns in each new generation, her name surfacing in books, in essays, in archival projects, in whispered comparisons when another woman dies violently and too soon. Her shadow flickers behind glass display cases in historical societies, or in a historian's notebook scribbled with half-legible quotes. She lingers in the smoke of America's early crime literature, in the legacy of yellow journalism, in the questions that still haunt us about whose stories get told—and how.

She remains, not as a myth, but as a memory interrupted.

To write about Helen Jewett is to walk through the fire again. To see the outline of a life through layers of bias, scandal, and moral judgment. To peel back the newsprint and look for the girl underneath.

Not the victim.

Not the symbol.

Just the girl.

The one who liked novels. The one who wanted love. The one who, on the last night of her life, locked her door—believing it would keep her safe.

She deserved better.

And remembering her clearly, without embellishment or shame, may be the closest thing we can offer in place of justice.

Not a conclusion.

But a reckoning.

Thankyou!

Thanks so much for reading. If you've made it this far, I truly appreciate you taking the time to dive into this story. I love exploring mysteries, conspiracies, and forgotten corners of history—and I'm just getting started. I'll be creating more books like this, and if you enjoyed the experience, I'd be thrilled to have your support. Whether that's by sharing the book, reaching out with your thoughts, or simply staying curious, it all means a lot. If you'd like to help support future projects, you can also do so through PayPal. Either way, thank you for being part of the journey.

Paypal.me   Check my other work on amazon

Appendices & References

Appendix A: Case Documents

Timeline of Events (1830–1836)

A condensed chronology based on contemporary news reports, survivor testimonies, police records, and trial transcripts:

- **1830–1832** — Dorcas Doyen (later Helen Jewett) begins her transformation from a well-educated Maine girl to a courtesan in Boston and later New York City.

- **1833–1835** — Helen works in various brothels, earning a reputation for wit, literacy, and selectiveness in her clientele.

- **January 1836** — Richard P. Robinson begins corresponding and visiting Helen under the alias "Frank Rivers."

- **April 9, 1836 (Evening)** — Helen is last seen alive by brothel residents. She retires to Room 3 at approximately 10:00 p.m.

- **April 10, 1836 (3:00–4:00 a.m.)** — Rosina Townsend reports smelling smoke and finds Helen's bed on fire. The body is discovered with a hatchet wound to the head.

- **April 10, 1836 (Morning)** — Richard Robinson is arrested after being linked by witness statement and circumstantial evidence (including cloak, handwriting).

- **May–June 1836** — The trial of Richard P. Robinson takes place in New York City. Newspapers, especially *The New York Herald*, cover the proceedings extensively.

- **June 2, 1836** — Robinson is acquitted after fifteen minutes of jury deliberation. The public response is sharply divided.

- **1837 and beyond** — Rosina Townsend disappears from public life. Robinson reportedly moves south and adopts a new identity. No one else is charged with the crime.

Witness Quotes (Trial and Inquest)

"These girls are not what they are made out to be, and neither are the gentlemen." — *Rosina Townsend, testifying in court*

"She looked beautiful even in death—her face was half-burned, but still you could see it." — *Unnamed brothel resident, 1836 police interview*

"The room was bolted from the inside. No man could have entered or left unseen." — *Officer John Norris, early responder to the scene*

"The girl was clever, not just pretty. She knew how to read men, how to read books." — *Sarah E. Leary, former acquaintance of Helen*

Room Layout Description (41 Thomas Street)
While no architectural drawings survive, police records and Rosina Townsend's testimony provide a functional layout:

- **Ground Floor** — Entry hall, Rosina Townsend's quarters, a parlor used for meeting clients.

- **Second Floor** — Rooms rented by the women: Room 3 (Helen's), Room 4 (another working girl), and a shared washing closet.

- **Back Stairwell** — Used for discretion, connecting bedrooms to rear exit.

- **Locks** — Each door had internal bolts. Helen's was found bolted from the inside.

Key Physical Evidence (Recovered from the Crime Scene)

- **Hatchet** — Bloodied blade, suspected murder weapon. No prints or ownership confirmed.

- **Burned Nightgown** — Scorched silk, partially covering the body. Suggests arson was secondary.

- **Silk Cloak** — Believed to belong to Robinson, identified by Rosina and brothel residents.

- **Letter Fragments** — Several partially burned letters found in Helen's room; handwriting possibly Robinson's.

- **Boot Impressions** — Light tracking from stairwell to rear door. No signs of forced entry.

Appendix B: Historical Context & Glossary
Glossary of 19th-Century American Legal and Social Terms

- **Coroner's Inquest** — A formal inquiry to determine cause of death, often held before trial to guide prosecution.

- **Courtesan** — A sex worker of relatively high status, often literate, well-dressed, and maintaining fewer clients.

- **Character Testimony** — Common in 19th-century trials; used to sway jury by elevating or degrading moral standing.

- **Yellow Journalism** — Sensationalistic news style that emerged prominently after Jewett's case but rooted in its reporting.

- **Moral Reform Societies** — Civic groups in the 1830s–40s that aimed to end prostitution and reform "fallen women."

Social and Legal Context of the Era

- **Status of Women in 1830s New York** — Women, particularly those in sex work, lacked legal standing. Their word in court was often considered unreliable unless corroborated.

- **Urban Crime** — The 1830s saw a spike in crime rates due to rapid urbanization. Policing systems were still informal.

- **Role of the Press** — Newspapers shaped trials as much as evidence did. Journalists like James Gordon Bennett turned court cases into serialized drama.

- **Class Tension** — Robinson's acquittal reflected tensions between the working class and a judicial system perceived to protect the elite.

Appendix C: Digital Companion Resources

These resources provide additional reading, visual references, and primary source archives.

Case-Related Archives

- *New York Court Records Archive* — Includes 1836 trial transcript and witness depositions.

- *Library of Congress – 19th Century American Crime Reports* — Features clippings and judicial documents related to Helen Jewett's murder.

- *Maine State Archives* — Genealogical records for Dorcas Doyen (Helen Jewett), including early census records.

Media and Journalism

- *New York Herald Archives* — Bennett's original 1836 reports on the case.

- *American Journalism History Review* — Analytical articles on the evolution of crime reporting, starting with Jewett's case.

- *The History of Sensationalism* (Columbia University Press) — Traces the roots of tabloid culture to the Jewett trial.

Scholarly and Public History Resources

- Patricia Cline Cohen, *The Murder of Helen Jewett* — Definitive biography and case history, University of California Press.

- *The American Antiquarian Society* — Holds broadsides, court sketches, and pamphlets related to the trial.

- *Gotham Center for New York City History* — Features essays on prostitution, reform, and crime in antebellum New York.

- *Women and Crime in 19th Century America* – Yale Digital Collections – Archival material related to sex work, moral policing, and public reaction.

References

Books and Memoirs

- Cohen, Patricia Cline. *The Murder of Helen Jewett: The Life and Death of a Prostitute in Nineteenth-Century New York*. Vintage Books, 1998.

- Gamber, Wendy. *The Notorious Mrs. Clem: Murder and Money in the Gilded Age*. Johns Hopkins University Press, 2016.

- Gilfoyle, Timothy J. *City of Eros: New York City, Prostitution, and the Commercialization of Sex, 1790–1920*. W. W. Norton & Company, 1992.

- Stansell, Christine. *City of Women: Sex and Class in New York, 1789–1860*. University of Illinois Press, 1987.

- Hughes, Kathryn. *Victorian Women: Lives and Letters*. Harper Perennial, 2005.

Academic Journals and Articles

- Balleisen, Edward J. "Law and Legal Institutions in the Lives of American Prostitutes, 1840–1940." *Law & Social Inquiry*, vol. 17, no. 2, 1992, pp. 307–331.

- Masur, Louis P. "Rites of Execution: Capital Punishment and the Transformation of American Culture, 1776–1865." *The Journal of American History*, vol. 77, no. 4, 1991, pp. 1219–1222.

- Reiss, Albert J. "The Police and the Public: Public Institutions and Private Behavior in 19th Century New York." *American Sociological Review*, vol. 25, no. 2, 1960.

Newspapers and Contemporary Press (1836)

- *The New York Herald*, April–June 1836 editions. James Gordon Bennett, editor.

- *The New York Sun*, April 11–12, 1836.

- *The New York Transcript*, coverage during trial week, May 1836.

- *The Evening Post* (New York), April 1836 crime scene reports.

- *The Daily Sentinel*, Maine editions 1834–1835, tracking early mentions of Dorcas Doyen.

Legal and Trial Records

- *People v. Richard P. Robinson*, Trial Transcript (1836), New York Court of Oyer and Terminer, New York County Archives.

- Coroner's Inquest Report: Death of Helen Jewett, April 1836. New York Municipal Coroner's Office Records.

- Police Docket Entry #3442: Statement by Rosina Townsend, April 10, 1836. Manhattan Police Archives.

- Grand Jury Indictment Docket, 1836 – Clerk of Courts, New York County Hall of Records.

Historical Societies and Archives

- New-York Historical Society – Helen Jewett Collection. Includes ephemera, trial notices, and broadsides.

- Library of Congress – 19th Century Crime Pamphlets Collection.

- Bowery Historical Preservation Archive – Prostitution and Police Control (1820–1870).

- Maine State Archives – Doyen Family Census Records, Temple and Farmington Townships.

- Columbia Rare Book & Manuscript Library – 19th-Century Sensationalist Journalism Archive.

Digital Companion and Online Archives

- Chronicling America – Library of Congress Newspaper Archive.

- The Avalon Project – Yale Law School: American legal documents and early courtroom procedures.

- Smithsonian Magazine – "How a Murder in a Brothel Changed American Journalism" (2013).

- The Gilder Lehrman Institute of American History – Resources on antebellum urban crime.

- The Victorian Web – Sections on morality, social norms, and class in the 1830s.

- JSTOR – Full access to 19th-century social history and legal proceedings.

- New York Public Library Digital Collections – Maps and city directories of Lower Manhattan, 1830s.

A Letter to the Reader

Dear Reader,

Thank you for walking with me through the alleyways and gaslit chambers of Helen Jewett's story.

This book wasn't written simply to chronicle a crime—it was written to confront the uneasy truth that justice doesn't always arrive. Helen's case, like so many others, reveals how quickly a woman's life can be sensationalized, moralized, and ultimately forgotten by the very society that once hung on every sordid detail.

Writing *The Unsolved Murder of Helen Jewett* meant returning to a world where silence was currency, where the law bent toward privilege, and where the value of a woman's life was weighed against the purity of her reputation. It meant looking at a locked room and asking not just who held the hatchet—but who held the power.

This was never just about a single night in 1836. It's about what we choose to believe. About how stories get told, who gets to tell them, and who vanishes in the telling.

You didn't just read this book. You excavated it. Page by page, you stepped into candlelit courtrooms and soot-stained brothels. You listened for the truths buried under editorials and hearsay. You gave Helen something she was denied in life: the dignity of being remembered without judgment.

If a name, a passage, or a theory lingered in your thoughts—if you found yourself whispering "what if" or wondering how many Helens never made the headlines—then this story has done its work. Not because we've solved it. But because we've refused to let it disappear.

Thank you for investigating with me. For honoring her name. And for understanding that remembering is its own form of justice.

With gratitude and resolve,

Ricky Indrawan

Printed in Dunstable, United Kingdom